Heroes P

JANUARY AND THE SEASON'S OVER

life in the Football League

Steve Phelps

First published in Great Britain in 2007 by
Heroes Publishing.
P.O. Box 1703, Perry Barr,
Birmingham B42 1UZ.

ISBN 0-9543884-7-X

–

EAN 9780954388478

Cover photo Steve Beauchampe

Printed by printondemand-worldwide.com

Acknowledgements

Just a few, in the hope they'll all buy lots of copies of this book......

Dad and Rich for their company over the years and their support always.

Adam and Mark for comedy value, Jan for the pre-match meals, Lauren, Gemma, Jim and Dee for their support.

Ade, Tony, Steve, Trotty, Will, Swifty, Sarah, Taylos, Tim, Kieran, Ricki, Cookie, Richie, Aidan, Danny, Iolo, Matt, Tony, Brian, Shaun and Martyn for the banter and all the text messages.

Kalvin, Sue and Gough for reading the rough draft.

Dave at Heroes for making it happen, Jim at VSP for pointing me in Dave's direction.

Steve Froggatt for kindly supplying the foreword.

Finally, to Emma for 12 great years. Aimee and Jolie for three of the most exhausting years I've ever known and for being wonderful daughters.

This book is for my mum who would have bought the first copy, sat down with a cuppa and pretended to enjoy it! Not bad eh, Mum?

Steve Phelps
Summer 2007

Foreword

During my time at Highfield Road I was always pleasantly surprised by the loyalty and passion displayed by the Sky Blues fans. Despite the team's lack of success over the years, they have kept coming back for more and never ceased to get behind their team. I'm sure this backing played a massive part in helping Coventry defy the odds and remain in the top flight for so long.

Now, whenever I return to the Ricoh I can see that many things have changed. It's a different ground, for a start. The playing staff are completely unrecognisable from the squad of which I was a part. And sadly, the division in which Coventry now play is a lower one - you can only work miracles for so long. But the Sky Blues support remains the same. They're passionate, committed, not always uncritical, but always remain devoted to their cause.

It's easy to follow one of the glamour sides. This book tells what it's like to support a club who, as the author says, rarely live up to expectations.

I've enjoyed it and I'm sure you will, too.

STEVE FROGGATT
COVENTRY CITY 1998-2001
www.stevefroggatt.com

Contents

Introduction

Let me hand out a warning: This book won't give you any indication of what it's like to support a successful, winning football team. It will certainly not portray what it's like to celebrate victory every Saturday night. Visits to the Millennium Stadium or the new Wembley are conspicuous by their absence, as are open-top bus parades around the city and millionaire takeover bids. Away days at Ashton Gate and St. Mary's top the bill, while Old Trafford and Anfield are seen only on television. There's no mention of multi-million pound transfer fees and five-figure wages don't exist.

Football League stadiums are rarely filled to capacity and the atmosphere suffers as a result. It was only back in 2001 when we were amongst the elite but now you never see us gracing the back pages, let alone the front ones.

What this book contains is the hope and expectation that maybe, just this once, a return to the Premiership will still be a possibility as May approaches. This hope and expectation always turns into frustration and disbelief, a pair of emotions frequently prevalent amongst football supporters.

During the top-flight years we were the final slot on Match of the Day, the two minute cameo prior to the credits. Drop down a division and now it's the Football League Review. For those of you unfamiliar with such low-level programming this is a goals-only highlights programme usually shown in the early hours of Wednesday morning. Cup runs and challenging for a European place are for others, while Match of the Day and Sky Soccer

Sunday as anything other than a neutral observer are a fading memory.

Although far from a trophy-laden tale, in my sky blue-tinted spectacled opinion it's a lot more interesting than following Chelsea or Arsenal. The inconsistencies and frustrations of a run of the mill lower league side ensure that you never know what's around the corner. There are many like me who've attended hundreds of football matches, yet victory provides only an occasional glint of light. Growing up in Coventry, 1980 saw my first visit to Highfield Road. For the last ten years I've lived near Bristol and pay for my match tickets through working in the travel industry. I'm a busy daddy to Aimee and Jolie, our two year-old twins, and the ninety-mile drive to the Ricoh ensures every match is an away game. While my life has changed over the years, not a lot has altered in the way my team have performed. We were usually a struggling top division side and now we're usually a struggling second tier one. Seventeen managers since my inauguration into the Sky Blue way of life tells its own story. I still have absolutely no control over anything they do and how they do it.

This book documents the years of support I've given to my team, contrasting the 2006-07 season with memories and anecdotes from years gone by. It also chronicles the inconsistency, frustration, bad decisions and bewilderment the club has given me in return. All of this for thousands of pounds of my cash and thousands of miles on the M5. There have been occasional terrific moments but they've been far outweighed by the habitual relegation struggles down the years and through the decades. You tend to remember the good times as, like a good woman, they come along rarely and you treasure the memories.

Each matchday experience of 2006-07 is detailed here regardless of my whereabouts: at the game, at work, at home, pub, on holiday or in the car. Wherever I am, a record of the ninety minutes is documented. When the goals go in and the final whistle blows it impacts on your everyday mood.

The emotions and reactions of the football supporter are often in synchronisation with the league position of their team. This is a tale fans up and down the country can identify with because I'm writing about them too. Season after season, game after game, the pattern is constant. Expectations are huge but the realism is massively deflating. If you're lucky and your kick-off time hasn't been messed around, come 3 o'clock on a Saturday, wherever you are, for ninety minutes plus stoppages all you can focus on is the match.

Chapter 1

Pre-season

May, June and July provide no stress on Saturday afternoons. There's no need to ensure you're accessible to the latest scores. The pressure's off and you can enjoy diversions such as beaches, Sainsbury's and IKEA. The only time you have to do anything stressful is when the fixtures come out and the itinerary from August to April is planned. Everything else is fitted around this essential guide to modern living to ensure that, yes my wife can go to the theatre with her mum, but only on a Friday and definitely not on a Saturday. Midweek is fine especially if we have a game, as I'll put my daughters to bed then join Jeff Stelling and company for the evening's entertainment.

There are no mood swings pre-season as there are no defeats to stomach and no dubious decisions to view. I don't have to ensure the kids are entertained while the Championship goals grace ITV and they can watch what they want with no Goals on Sunday to work the morning routine around. No late winners come through on Final Score at 4.58 and the tension in the office is reduced, with teletext usage considerably lower.

Speculation is, of course, rife during the summer. Who've we signed? More like who we've lost out on and who we'd like to sign but have no chance whatsoever. Pre-season sets the optimism/pessimism levels for the forthcoming campaign. On hearing the opening fixtures, my Manchester City-supporting mate Tony opined via text message:

"We need to get something out of the first six games or we're stuffed!"

This was five minutes after the fixtures were released at the end of June.

You automatically view the opening day, Boxing Day and the final day, to see where you'll be setting off on the right foot, planning the Christmas meet and lifting the coveted trophy. The work roster is planned up until next May and you already know the games you can attend. Social life is dictated by working in the unpredictable travel industry, with one weekend in three off ensuring meticulous planning. Soccer AM repeats are shown on Saturday mornings while Tim and Helen have the summer off. Phone-in programmes are redundant with no 606 for the drive home from work. Instead there's Masters Football on Sky, test matches, Wimbledon and the latest transfer sagas amongst Premiership clubs to fill the sporting pages.

We have our own Skytext page number to keep up with the latest news but they're just more reports of newspaper headlines snippets than anything else this time of year. And we rarely make the headlines even during the season.

The opening day brings people out of the woodwork who you haven't had contact with for ages. The start of a new season unites football supporters and associates certain friends with the world's greatest game. The previous season is forgotten about already. Southend fan Ricki, awash with enthusiasm after two successive promotions, greets me with: *"Good luck for the new season, I'm off to Roots Hall."* This is the first of many texts I'll receive throughout the season from supporters around the country. Come November his mood will be different. After a newly promoted outfit gets a few early wins, communication will cease then there's less and less enthusiasm as they lose their fourth game on the trot. Southend have endured many years in the doldrums but their time is now and their success is to be enjoyed because it won't last.

Next up is Charlton mate Aidan offering the pessimistic option: *"Charlton will struggle - not enough quality."* I'm inclined to agree.

As some of the lads follow Premiership sides the start of our season is immaterial to them. They never comment on how we will fare as, in simple terms, the Championship doesn't exist to them apart from a brief debate about who might go up, and that's not going to be us.

City have financial reward for the season's opener, being sponsored by Sky Sports for the day we welcome last season's Premiership whipping boys Sunderland. I'm completely relaxed and looking forward to our new campaign with the most optimism I can honestly recall since 1997-98. That season we ended up eleventh, with Dion Dublin the Premiership's joint top scorer alongside Michael Owen. Then we sold him to Villa.

This time I'm sticking my neck out on a top six finish, which has never happened in my lifetime whatever the division. With ten new signings possessing younger legs, new-found defensive strength and pace in midfield I firmly believe the corner has been turned, but football supporting is as predictable as the world of travel.

Before the Premiership starts, 606 is a delight with no whinging Spurs or West Ham supporters demanding to know why their club isn't top of the league, or some Manchester United moron from Hertfordshire complaining that having to play Watford is no proper preparation for their upcoming Champions League programme and the Premier League should do something about it. We have ecstatic Hereford and Colchester supporters delighted with their start to the campaign. These fans enthuse about what football is really about. A world away from the Premiership and a world I definitely prefer now I've seen both sides.

Bookmakers are a major player in broadcasting choice. As soon as the odds are released and the fixtures in print, Sky releases the live schedules. The favourites instantly receive appropriate airplay and Birmingham and West Brom are tipped for an instant return. The plan within the two establishments is to avoid the loss of their parachute payments and Sky Sports subsequently allocates them August/September live slots, featuring each side on the eve of the campaign. They seem taken in by the hype but I'm less gullible. Blues will struggle in the way we did, as the expectation is massive. After four years out of the lower tier they believe they have a right to play in the top league but it's not quite that straightforward. Stars leave to be replaced by inferior quality and those that remain fail to raise their game in the frenetic pace of the Championship.

Relegated sides face cup finals every game with the opposition upping their standards when the fixture comes around. Fans quickly become frustrated as to secure automatic promotion no more than ten games can be lost. Or maybe that's just us. We're 14/1 for the title and haven't been seventh favourite for any league in my lifetime. A good play-off bet? I reckon.

Pre-season I've been extremely confident and expecting this to be the season. No, honest. This time I really mean it. The night before the opener I'm already working out what will happen in the initial clump of five games prior to the first of many international breaks. Realism immediately kicks into my thinking as we must beat Sunderland on day one. If we lose to Saints and Cardiff like we normally do away after winning the opener then Leicester on Sky is the six pointer. Already.

This is followed by the trip to Humberside, therefore, losing three out of the first five is not play-off form and leaves only a handful of losses permitted in the remaining 41 fixtures. Christ, I prefer pre-season as my thoughts in May and June are always optimistic. Suddenly I'm looking into a variety of permutations and it will reach the stage where other fixtures are checked to see how far we drop down the table if we lose. This is a usual tactic me and many others employ and will happen after a dozen games.

This negative thinking is never far away and the worrying aspect from this last paragraph is that we haven't even kicked a ball yet. I've checked the car over and the petrol gauge is looking healthy. The oil's fine and DVD players are strapped to the headrests to occupy the kids. My alarm is set for seven to get washed before the twin siren is heard and the morning turns into a hive of feeding, loading the car and getting out the door by 9.30 for the journey to the Ricoh.

All this for Sunderland at home.

Chapter 2
Off to a flyer

Unlike a Saturday match our Sky-influenced Sunday has the motorway clear with an earlier than usual start for a 1.30 kick off. Overloaded cars returning from stressful family holidays in the south-west congest the services with surfboards and suitcases strapped to the roof. Strensham services near Worcester sport pensioners on a wild day out having a loo break. They clog up the queues asking for a coffee or tea. The words 'latte' or 'cappuccino' are foreign to their ears as they only want a nice cup of Tetley and a rich tea. That is, the ones willing to "*pay them prices*". The rest use the toilets and sit in the café area with their flasks and wrapped sandwiches.

While we sup our coffees the peace of other drinkers is shattered by the singing of nursery rhymes and excitement of a new place. The people in question are with us and nearly two years old, having a great time. Costa Coffee atmosphere is fun for them but the Ricoh is my domain. As we arrive at my Dad's house, a ten-minute drive from the home of football, the mood is mixed. Seasonal expectations vary as we debate the coming season and views range from third to tenth place finishes. My brother Rich is the sceptic, or could he be the realist? We have the full compliment for the opener with t-shirt weather prevailing today, a real rarity with football. None of us are under six foot two and the Rover's suspension takes the full force as we cram into the back.

The routine hasn't altered down the years as on hearing the engine growl into life Coventry & Warwickshire Radio brings us the team news and preview. Presented by the same guys for years, they also host the phone-in after the game. It's rarely been a positive programme but the back end of last season and an eventual eighth place finish saw the first shoots of optimism since Thatcher was in power.

To park at the Ricoh incurs an annual fee of £240 but common sense prevails so we settle for a £5 space in the Foleshill Social Club. The locals are crammed in, playing the first house of bingo with the cigarette smoke billowing out the open windows as we arrive. The Ricoh Arena is situated next to the 'largest Tesco in Europe' and Sunderland fans illegally cram the car park with red and white everywhere.

The walk to the ground gives us time to debate the pre-season purchases with the emphasis on youth and pace. As we approach the concourse surrounding our highly impressive stadium the sight of queues is something we are not familiar with. Mild heart flutters ensue, the key thought being, *"Will we get in on time?"* This has never happened before, as you never queue to get into a City match. It's unheard of yet there's obviously a reason as we haven't sold that many tickets. True to form the innovative credit card entrance system has failed the opening test and queues are building twenty minutes before kick-off. Fortunately common sense prevails and initiative, or was it fan pressure, sees the disabled access doors opened to allow us all in safely.

Pre-match entertainment has never been embraced by our club and the Sky Blue Crew have 'performed' dance routines for years. Particularly badly. The pre-match entertainer from funky local radio welcomes away fans then turns to the home support. Half of them are still sinking Carlsberg and demolishing nasty pies in the concourse area. His remit is to work the crowd into a frenzy prior to kick off. Usually there's the odd clap and cheer but today is different. Local chart-topping early 80's band King pump out over the PA shortly before the teams' arrival with their greatest hit selection Love and Pride. It catches the crowd on the back foot but achieves the desired effect.

The Ricoh is not full and the round trip of 400 miles has only appealed to 3,000 Sunderland fans. Many others are so used to losing they prefer to stay at home and watch it in the local for the cost of a few pints. Fair enough; the same could apply to me but you have to be at the opening game. New signings receive a tumultuous welcome on announcement of the starting line-ups. How this can change as the season progresses.

The pre-match huddle generates a fantastic roar and the City fans are well behind the team here. Initial vibes are good and expectation higher than normal due to our pre-season additions. We watch from the NTL stand located opposite the dug-outs. Rarely empty, the stand is segregated into pricing zones with ours costing £23. A Burberry-free area, the people around us appear normal but this is simply an initial impression. By that I mean they're there for the football and watching their team; some with their kids, others in groups.

Our group of five is like the World Cup panel. Throughout the match our observations are continuous and criticisms scathing. We could all do better ourselves. In our considered opinion numerous players' seasons are over after one game. The ref puts whistle to lips and this is it. The Coventry City promotion season is underway.

At half-time I'm barefoot as the Ricoh is roasting, a real swelter shelter. To wear t-shirt and shorts to a football match in England occurs only at the first and last home games. The rest of the season sees us moving through light jackets to thick coats, complimented with obligatory fashion accessory hats and scarves. Approaching Christmas the floodlights are on by half-time and it's pitch black when you leave the ground from then until the end of January. Then it's freezing until the end of March, which is why the opening day encounter is always one of the best.

Hotter than ever today; it's humid enough in the stands and with frequent breaks in play the players are regularly guzzling on the pitch. There's no point eating pies, so the main half-time requirement is bottled water all round as we discuss the goalless first 45. Coming from a goal down to win a game is not a feat we often see at Coventry; you resign yourself to defeat and may as well go home once the opposition have taken the lead. Today the gods are smiling on us as two strikes in seven minutes send the Ricoh into raptures and an opening day success is gained.

However, we've got to be careful here as it's easy to get swept away. Sunderland look poor; the idea of having Niall Quinn as chairman/manager is a novel one but it doesn't look like the north-east is yet ready to be in the vanguard of such footballing innovation. We didn't play that well but still took the points. The unpredictability of football rears its delightful head yet again as we normally end up on the receiving end of such reverses. I apologise for my permanently pessimistic thoughts but this comes with the territory.

A first for us occurred on the short drive back to Dad's house. With knees round our chins and legs stuck together with sweat the car snakes along as we leave the ground. It's bumper-to-bumper for miles. We had to wait to get in and out. How times are changing or is it simply down to poor transport links around a newly built, out of town stadium?

My regular Monday read, The Game sports section of the Times, described Operation Premiership, the three-year plan designed to return us to the megabucks era. Optimism is racing but I just hope we're all not getting just a bit too excited based on Sunday's initial impression.

The season I was born, 1973-74, saw industrial strife as prime minister Ted Heath took on the coal miners in an industrial dispute. 'Strife' perfectly summarises my lifetime supporting Coventry City. At the beginning of every season expectations are raised only to be dashed by the turn of the year. The focus towards the end of the season is usually survival. Occasionally there's consolidation, yet our campaigns rarely canter to a conclusion. Success-wise, January draws the curtain on silverware. February, March, April and May see the season drawn out to the last few games. Our eyes are firmly fixed on the league table and our rivals' results. Survival is greeted with celebration until the next time and the play-offs are always for others.

Manchester United were relegated at the end of my inaugural season. Their place in the elite was taken by Carlisle United. Leeds were champions and we finished in 16th position. The following season saw Derby County win the league with Stoke fifth and Chelsea relegated. This is how I know that sometime, don't know when, our time will come.

***

"Have we missed the turn off for Newbury?"

This question was asked by Ade, a Rugby lad living in Bristol and my chauffeur down to the south coast. Too right we had. We had a sneaking feeling we were off track as we passed Guildford and Aldershot signs. An urgent detour via Bracknell and down country lanes at breakneck speed saw us back on the deserted M4 and heading back to Bristol.

It had all started so well as, cutting a swathe through rush hour traffic, we reached Southampton in plenty of time for a pre-match pie and plastic pint. The impressive St Mary's was awash with red and white stripes, its inner concourse packed with City fans quaffing a last-minute Carlsberg and similar football ground fare. With masses of City fans arriving just shy of kick-off from various destinations they catch the Saints ground staff on the back foot as an impressive following of 1,500 roar the side onto the pitch. As with our empire, the corners are empty.

Saints are celebrating the demise of their former regime and the crowd are whipped into a frenzy by the appearance on the pitch of noted double-act Channon and Ball. The first half begins fairly open but ends with our hosts running us ragged. This continues into the second half until an innocent tackle is punished, quite literally. Their teen left-back repeats his opening day party piece and strikes one into the top corner to leave our heads bowed. Unbelievable. We're right behind the wonder strike and the damn thing doesn't deviate an inch. Gareth Bale, another in the Southampton conveyor belt of talent that includes Theo Walcott and, a few years earlier, Matt le Tissier. Why can't we bring through kids like that?

The one consolation is that he won't be playing against us next season. The days when promising youngsters were happy to improve their game in the lower divisions have long gone – he'll be off to the Premier League just as soon as his agent works out his percentage. Our initial reaction for now, though, was should a 'keeper be beaten from that distance?

The three sub trick fails to make an immediate impact until a sniper appears and drops their easily-felled Polish striker Grzegorz Rasiak in our area. With two minutes to go it's game over thanks to the referee who has influenced the result with two incorrect calls. I bet he doesn't have the hundred-mile plus drive home at this time of night. He'll be tucked up in the Travelodge and drive back in the morning with his conscience clear. Thanks ref, our subsequent detour adds insult to injury.

Knowing my alarm is ready for action at 6am, my walk in the door five hours earlier chuffs me to bits. One final thing to do before lights out is to catch the goals just to make sure I was right. Yes, they were dodgy calls, which is more frustrating but self-satisfying at the same time. It just proves my Sky Blue tinted version of events in the heat of the moment is correct. I don't need action replays even if the officials do.

Southend have enjoyed glory with successive promotions and Scunthorpe look set to follow in their footsteps. Success can be defined as accomplishing an aim. I just want us to win something because it's been twenty long years since we triumphed at Wembley. I was twelve years old and like most people at the time I sported a wedge haircut, wore bleached drainpipe jeans, Fred Perry tops and the crowning glory, white socks. The Chicago Bears were recently defeated in Superbowl 41. They'd last appeared in the showpiece game in Superbowl 19 so it can be done. My dad waited until he was 42 to saviour the cup success. If you search long and hard there are teams less successful than us: Rochdale.

Gutted. Only forty miles from our house is Ninian Park, it's a quick hop down the M4 for those going to the game but I'm on the M32 on the way to the centre of Bristol. I've got to work, but access to the scores is easy. Final Score and teletext break the bad news as the afternoon progresses and while the game of football is in progress the day is put on hold. Half-time comes as a welcome relief with us still goalless. While discussing the finer points of following inconsistent sides with Man City season ticket holder Tony, the **Cardiff 0-0 Coventry** teletext icon suddenly illuminates to show **Cardiff 1-0 Coventry** with eleven minutes remaining. The 'phone went down as teletext was substituted by Final Score. I expected to be greeted by Ray Stubbs and the panel discussing our late comeback, yet a shock awaited me. Athletics! Pre-Premiership all you get is any goals scored at 4.55 (so that's none then) and then it quickly flicks to the classified check. I've had enough of this Premiership bias, ever since we got relegated. A quick look (after only three games) at page 325 on teletext confirms the lower half of the table for us already. One of these days we'll start well and sit in the top half, pushing towards the play offs. Level on points with Southend, the Ricoh Arena comfort blanket is sadly conspicuous by its absence again.

The drive home took in 606 with gripes and groans from extremely disgruntled Ipswich fans. Three straight defeats, a rookie manager and no cash to strengthen the side has led to the inevitable clamour for the manager's head. Sounds familiar in seasons previous with the reigns of Gary McAllister and Roland Nilsson who were great players yet found themselves thrust into a no-win situation. Now we're only £25 million in debt compared to the £60 million millstone dangled around the aforementioned gentlemens' necks. Buoyant from a terrific start to the season, the Plymouth travelling army returning from Sunderland peppered the airwaves.

Such a refreshing change, I was thinking, as I headed home until we came to so and so from Cheshire who wanted to complain about Manchester United's lack of firepower. I ask you. Having just watched them defeat Sevilla 3-0 in a pre-season stroll he interrupts our show and their season has yet to even start! Who cares that they only have Saha and Rooney up front, let's get the real fans back on the show and get rid of the perennial whinge merchants who wouldn't know an unsuccessful season if it reared up and bit them on the proverbial.

The show is Premiership-free this time of year. At least let us have the slot to ourselves as we normally don't stand a chance of getting through the complainants once the top-flight season gets underway. If there was a lower league 606 it would be more realistic than the show is at present. Premiership fans live in a world of their own, a complete dreamland.

Since 1974 Carlisle, Hartlepool and Torquay have all achieved and no doubt thoroughly enjoyed the rare delight of promotion success within the Football League. A 46-game magical marathon with the defeats very rare, draws consolidating and victories in abundance. With goals raining in and Scrooge-like defending, attendances soar and the enthusiasm remains at fever pitch. The success didn't last for long but at least it happened. It lasted nine fabulous months, life never felt so good and your team were simply the best. Carlisle's fans, in September 1974, saw their team sit proudly on top of the old division one with victory at Chelsea. Moments of glory and achievement are to be savoured.

To witness a season with a century of points and 30-odd wins is the campaign of dreams. For the elite it's expected, defeat unthinkable. For us and many other sides it's an unprecedented delight. Most certainly hoped for and dreamt of, never ever expected but fully appreciated. Since 1980 our two most notable turning points could not contrast more. That wonderful day at

Wembley in 1987 defeating the once mighty Spurs after extra time and the top flight relegation at Villa Park in 2001. The drop had been avoided more times than I care to remember prior to that fateful, inevitable day. It's never been boring, occasionally brilliant, yet always immensely frustrating. It still is.

Chapter 3

Once a selling club
always a selling club

Birmingham's fifth bid for our leading light, Gary McSheffrey, is finally accepted by the City board and he's off for £4million. The only players we've sold for more in the last six years are Robbie Keane and Chris Kirkland. And so the debt reduces from £25 million to a mere £21 million, in theory. In reality the realisation is quite different. Some of it will be used to re-strengthen, some to appease the bank.

McSheffrey will be missed. He's done well for us and he wanted to stay but football's a business where money speaks volumes. The response is interesting:

"I bet you buy Eastwood with the money"

"Coventry in for some chingers!"

Fair enough, the money will strengthen the team but he'll be difficult to replace. There'll be an outcry at the next home game but not to the extent of Andy Cole's move from Newcastle to Manchester United. Micky Adams won't be out on the steps outside the ground appeasing the hordes of disgruntled fans because we don't have any. The leading critics will attack the Operation Premiership plan. Ambition is pronounced then, within weeks, instantly denounced with the stroke of a pen.

Only when the final whistle blows and you've won can you enjoy being a football supporter. On the walk to the game the chatter is expectant, with match predictions eagerly lauded. The comfort zone is before and after the game. Decisions taken during the next ninety minutes are completely out of your control. For the next week, until the next game, the feelgood factor is prevalent. I'm a supporter of a wonderfully inconsistent, occasionally terrific, rarely boring yet immensely frustrating Championship side. The relief when the game ebds victorious is palpable. Viewed through rose-tinted specs the performance is relatively immaterial. The result is the key and for the duration of the game nerves, tension, anxiety and pressure grip every supporter of every football team the length and breadth of the country.

Chelsea fans feel the pressure, as did Manchester United fans in the nineties and Liverpool before them. The key difference is that I don't really expect us to win. A win is a bonus and fans of the aforementioned teams expect to win and win well. A draw is disappointing for them and defeat unthinkable. For me defeat is expected, a draw not too bad and winning is just great. Saturday evening or the next day at work has that feelgood factor. It's out with the takeaway and the bottle of wine, even the chores appear not so bad. Reading about a victory is so much more appealing than a reverse. The Sunday papers are anticipated instead of feared.

"Why did you sell McSheffrey?" rang out around the Ricoh as we laboured to a goalless bore draw live on Sky with Leicester the visitors. Again chosen by Sky to head their ratings we'll be lucky to receive another invite after this showing. Summed up by Foxes fan Will: *"How dull was that? You can buy me a beer anyway."* So I lose out on both counts.

As the game was played on the Friday night it gave me no time to get there after work. Sky viewing is interesting, as is watching other people's opinions of your team. Your wife witnesses you hollering at the television, deciding she'd rather have a bath, or receiving texts from your mates. Work colleague Trotty, whose grasp of written English isn't all it could be, furnishes my Nokia with: *"Wot do u expect? Their shite!"* This from a man who follows Somerset at cricket.

The final twenty minutes showed promise with the addition of width and pace. Too many of Adams's favourites are gracing the team at present. Our full-backs are the obvious (to me anyway) weak link. We give the ball away too easily, which might explain why we haven't scored for three games. This always frustrates me early on in the season. Why can't we bang in the goals and see our strikers topping the scoring charts for a change? Because we fail to give them any decent service, that's why.

It's fair to say that football supporting is all-consuming, an obsession for some, and it can take over your life. At times gripping, it's a ruling passion in the lives of people up and down the country. You have to wonder who can sit there and actually enjoy watching their team. Viewing the match as a neutral is far more enjoyable.

I enjoy watching Coventry at 4-0 up, without question. 3-0 up, usually. At 2-0 there's no way you can sit back and enjoy the moment. This enjoyment factor is a rarity, and for us it happens maybe once a season. You savour the moment, as edge of the seat stuff is the norm. We never leave the ground early as there's always too much riding on the conclusion of the match, usually with us chasing the game. As a neutral observer there's no pressure and no expectation with not a care in the world. Time stands still when your team are winning, but races away rapidly if you're losing. Rapidly is our norm.

Walking into school and latterly work on a Monday morning after yet another defeat for twenty-odd years has rarely been enjoyable. When victory happens everything is so much better and this feeling lasts until the next game. Then we go through it all again. Your life 'pause' button is depressed between 3.00 and 4.55ish or from 7.45 to 9.35ish.

Spending the week in remotest Devon was a throwback to living at home in the pre-Sky era. We had no mobile signal and certainly no Sky dish. West Country News (Plymouth and Torquay) was the only source of information and I was rubbing the remote's batteries to coax extra life out of them, praying they'd last until the game had concluded. With just enough coverage for a teletext reception and no mobile link until back in

Bideford, our Carling Cup first round clash at Hereford was one game I could turn down. Hereford are freshly promoted from the Conference, after all.

Chauffeur Ade offered his services to Edgar Street. I was tempted but it wouldn't have gone down too well with my ladies so I politely declined, knowing we'd win convincingly. After the bedtime routine I returned downstairs into our oak-beamed lounge with ten minutes gone. Full of hope I was expecting the goals to flicker through at regular intervals. A quick manoeuvre of the ageing remote control onto the latest teletext teleprinter scores revealed very little goal action. Not trusting my team whatsoever, page 319 (H-S) Carling cup scores was sourced and there it was. My Coventry City levels of trust completely vindicated. **Hereford 1 Coventry 0**. After only one minute!

I knew there'd be no text abuse with no signal so relaxed for a while. We'll be sure to equalise shortly and lead by half-time. Keeping up to speed on goalflashes with my wife watching UK Bikini Guide was negotiated via the commercial breaks. Approaching nine o'clock we were still in arrears. BBC1's Post Office drama Sorted began with the in-screen update flashing at the bottom of the screen. (My wife failed to notice). Concentrating on the final episode of the drama is tricky when your mind is hundreds of miles away. I knew deep down we were trailing when up flashed **D Adebola 59**. What it also flashed up was **Hereford 2 Coventry 1**. My initial relief then turned into agitation that we were on course for another embarrassing reverse at the hands of a lower league team, yet again. I've lost count of the number of times this has happened; we almost expect it, like a lamb to the slaughter. The clock was ticking so much quicker as we were trailing. This agitation turned to thorough annoyance extremely quickly with the appearance of **Hereford 3-1 Coventry**.

With 25 minutes remaining I feared for more. My mentality is such that I expect us to concede further rather than fight back into the game. At the end of Sorted I checked page 319 to see if the in-vision information was wrong. Alas, no. The score was indeed right.

Along with a number of other Championship sides we bowed out, excruciatingly, to a league two (old division four) side. They came up through the Conference play-off final in May. At home I would have scrolled through all the reports on the defeat to find out why we lost. Here, in the back of beyond, page 305 gave a one-page report praising Hereford while ITV showed Plymouth's capitulation to Walsall.

With my mobile safely tucked up asleep for the night, I knew when it awoke the following day it would vibrate for Britain and so it did. Here is the chain of the previous evening's events via texts that I received queuing for a pasty in Barnstaple:

7.43pm. Ade: *"Your missing out, edgar st is a palatial stadium, st marys is shit compared to this."*

Interestingly enough he failed to text again from the terrace.

8.40pm. Rich (half-time): *"Fantasy league I am 119th overall!"*

No mention of the game.

8.52pm. Ricki (just gone 3-1 down): *"Whats happening to you boys?"*

11.28pm. Tony (Man City loyal, chucking-out time): *"Mate just seen league cup scores- Hereford? - Glad I never put money on Cov to get promoted."*

Reading the Times for the coverage of the previous night's ties, I've concluded the paper is a Premiership/Champions League dedication and a Championship exclusion zone. Not only were the scores notable by their absence, but they failed to even squeeze in a classified check. Not to worry though, as the tennis and baseball made it to print. Surely deadlines can allow for the tension and glamour of the Carling Cup first round? If Champions League qualifying ties kicking off at the same time can make the back page then surely we can receive a tiny bit of coverage?

A similar precedent is set with teletext coverage. Any news outside of the Premiership transfers/gossip features in the News in Brief section. No longer do we command a dedicated page number, we're blended in with our fellow lower league clubs and exclusivity reigns for the Premiership. It really is a world apart.

More importantly, that's now three straight reverses on the road. This aspect alone will hinder any promotion push. It hampered us last season and away from the Ricoh we just cannot perform. The mentality is wrong when we're out of our comfort zone. The season is turning sour like they all have since that fateful day in 2001.

Chapter 4

To Hull and back

Football supporting is one of the strongest relationships you can forge and it's a wholly one-way experience. Loyalty and dedication are paramount yet you get very little in return. No thanks, no pat on the back, just grief, heartache, sleepless nights, humiliation, frustration and a severe lack of loving.

Until 1995-96 the journey to Highfield Road took a few minutes. The opposition determined the time we left the house, parking being the key issue. Liverpool or Manchester United was an early departure, the reason being loads of Coventry locals were there for the away team. Pinching the best parking spots they sit amongst the home fans for their once a season treat, inconveniencing our Saturday routine.

Southampton, Wimbledon or Norwich at ease. No locals follow them so parking was a breeze. Plenty of time to read the programme and catch the line-ups. You never get queues driving to or from our games. Cod and chips on the way home after Sports Report then off to the newsagent to collect The Pink to read the match report. That was matchday.

A near five-hour crawl negotiated back from Devon, the afternoon was spent unpacking and stretching the spinal column in the company of Jeff Stelling and the wisecracking panel. A superstitious lawn mow at half-time influenced the result in no way, the clamour for CBeebies rebuffed. Hull away is the kind of game you should win based on the teams' respective paths over the last few years. I'm not patronising, just realistic. Come 4.45 we're still the only goalless fixture in the division and we're not even one of the selected games for coverage at regular intervals. We feature as an afterthought, if there's a goal they'll bring in their reporter at the KC Stadium. That's the key word to listen out for.

Let's be honest, it doesn't stand out. I'm expecting a red card or something daft to happen, such is the sheer unpredictability of football. We love the fact that every game is so different than the previous one. We expect the unexpected but it still throws up shocks. Suddenly, something daft does happen. With five minutes left we get a goal and win the game. It's the kind of away triumph of which you need around eight or nine if you've got any chance of going up.

When the name **Kevin Thornton 85** appeared I was halfway through reading The Snail and the Whale, my bargaining tool for distracting my daughters from the TV off button. While buried in the pages I only caught the name. I failed to see the teams and score appear. I looked back at the book then instantly returned my trance to the screen to confirm my disbelief. Group hugs all round. My girls didn't have a clue what I was rejoicing for. They simply raised their arms and cheered like daddy did.

***

July 1995. I met Emma. Our first date to Streatham Odeon revealed that she was from the West Country, 100 miles from Highfield Road. I didn't even know where it was on the map. This left me working out how this relationship would dovetail with my other relationship. I soon packed up my Lotto sports bag and headed down the M5 to Bristol after we left university.

Ten years on, the 200-mile round trip to Coventry has become routine. Due to my work we travel up in the Renault Scenic squad carrier every third weekend with Aimee and Jolie, our car crammed with toddler toys. Visits remain geared around the fixture list.

Five games into the season and it's time to take stock. Time to evaluate the initial clump of fixtures and prepare for the next five games before the international break. The transfer window slammed shut at the end of August and we have to wait until January for the re-open signs to appear. For the second time in as many months we signed a player for £1 million, Leon McKenzie from Norwich. He joins Elliott Ward in raising the club's profile as the bar of ambition is again lifted. The McSheffrey sale still lingers but the signings made since his departure will be awaited with bated breath. Thirteenth position can be changed to top five if we defeat Norwich after the international break.

Emma and I worked out an understanding after initially deciding to sample each other's interests, as you do when you first meet someone and are trying to impress. You do all the right things and, most importantly, say all the right things. She went to five Premiership games and called it quits. Likewise I haven't been to the theatre in a long time. She no longer asks me about the offside rule, I never ask how long it is until the curtain comes down. Her knowledge about football has improved dramatically but more out of having it repeatedly drummed into her via the Sky dish and the increase of football celebrities in life in general. In years to come Aimee and Jolie will hopefully fly the flag and sit with me at the Ricoh. The fact that they are free until seven years old plays no part in my thinking or the fact that my season ticket would be cheaper than where I sit now.

***

The journey to my dad's house only took us three hours. Thanks go out to the Range Rover that broke down on the slip road to the A46 and the perennial roadworks prevalent in Coventry. Breaking halfway at Strensham services it was plain to see the Premiership roadshow was back in town. The increased volume of traffic saw Manchester United-filled vehicles everywhere. All in their replica tops, the car next to ours sporting a Yeovil Town FC sticker. Do they only watch United when Yeovil are away?

Parking up at the social club the attendant was proud to highlight the newly-laid surface, and bingo again prevailed inside. A scorching day, the cut across Tesco's car park saw us enter the Ricoh, or try to. Last time out the card swipe system malfunctioned, this time the turnstile refused to rotate. With the turnstile operator frantically flicking the switch my initial thought was if this all tallies up the crowd will be approaching 40,000, such was the vigour of his clicking. Eventually we were through. My next thought was good job we weren't entering Old Trafford with the size of their crowds.

Norwich again turned out a decent following, resplendent in their canary yellow shirts. Chants of *"Delia's Barmy Army"* rang out all afternoon, their eight-hour round trip not one I envied. Unfortunately for them we dominated and won 3-0 with well-crafted goals and a resolute, watertight defence. With twenty minutes remaining we were in the position of not being perched on the edge of our seat. No hanging on until the final whistle sounded this time. It felt, though, like we weren't getting value for money. It was all too easy. People were leaving before the end and not just Canaries sufferers. When the fourth official raised the board for stoppages the sound of seats flipping upwards was clearly audible and a good quarter of the crowd had departed by the time the Norwich contingent were put out of their misery. Surely our diehards should have been there at the end to salute the performance? Is beating the traffic really that important?

Football games only last for ninety and a few more minutes. If you've paid £23 then get your money's worth. I know congestion outside the ground is still a problem but you can't make that much headway by leaving a few minutes early. We moan enough when we play badly and lose so why can't we enjoy the rare good times and show appreciation to the team? One Norwich fan didn't take the defeat lying down, unlike his side. Displaying his rather large gut for all to see, it welcomed the chant, *"When did you last see your dick?"* There was no reply to that.

A final note as we sat in the car on the way home when the local phone-in brings Alan to the airwaves. Alan complains that our substitutions at 3-0 up were negative. We had no threat and sat back. No, Alan, you're completely wrong. We shut up shop, secured the points and saved legs for Tuesday's visit to Ipswich. The problem is that the situation is so rare we're unsure how to deal with it. Tactical common sense is rarely shown, so how can we be expected to understand when the situation is foreign to us?

I've noticed when we lose the text and phone abuse is immediate. When we win there's no contact at all. Only Man City Tony responds with the following, which neatly sums up the day:

"Super Cov - Who needs McSheffrey?"

Very true. The fans and players seem to have got over the sale, finally. Today has lifted not only spirits but also the team into the top half of the table. Page one of teletext gratefully received. One page nearer to the Premiership. We've now won more games than we've lost. It's been a while since we could say that.

Chapter 5

Top half for a change

I go to the Ricoh with dad, Rich and step-brothers Adam and Mark. We don't make all the games but put on a good appearance when work, cash flow and the train networks permit. You see groups of lads sat together at games but that didn't happen with me. It was difficult to find someone who supported Coventry, and this in a school two miles from the city centre.

My schoolmates followed the top teams as what was the point in supporting us? They could catch the bus to Highfield Road once a season to see their heroes win convincingly. There's no glory attached to Coventry. We fail to attract the top players and always have done. Once a selling club, always a selling club.

Only 5% of the city (population 305,000) supports the Sky Blues. While I was at school Liverpool and Manchester United were the flavours. Only the teachers followed their local teams. It's much better for your street cred to follow the elite.

Tearing home from work, collecting wife and kids, bathing kids and feeding wife the clock turned 8.15pm. As the remote turned on Sky Sports News the built-in negative thoughts I possess while following City kicked in. In a similar vein to the Hereford shambles I had to comb the scores to ensure we hadn't conceded prior to me tuning in. Half-time came and went. While I sat there working out the permutations of win, lose or draw, Rob McCaffery panned to Portman Road. You just knew we'd conceded. Then to cap it all I lose custody of the remote and Supernanny rears her delightful head.

Being a football fan there's always a Plan B in your locker. Out with the laptop and straight into bbc.co.uk/football. The live video score printer is my saviour tonight. With an hour gone I'm flicking between the live text from the game and then back to the printer. Suddenly, the video printer relays **Ipswich 1 Coventry 1 Ward 71**. And the world is such a better place. Clicking icons manically between the live text at the game and the football scores as they appear, the pendulum appears to be swinging heavily towards a Sky Blue victory. I can only see one outcome here. Genuinely. We are so on top of the game it's only a matter of time. And then, inevitably, Ipswich take the lead with six minutes to go. Bollocks. Typical City. We never get late goals to win games like other sides, even against the ones who claim that letting in late goals against the run of play is typical of them. It's only City whom the gods have it in for in this way.

The clock runs down and I'm working out the new league table already to see where we fall to. It transpires we move down to 11th, as results have gone for us. I shouldn't be looking at other sides' results this early in the campaign but the constant struggle in seasons gone by has me automatically looking at the lower reaches of the table. Our form in recent seasons has even the most optimistic City fan looking on the negative rather than positive. For us to be in the top half so early in the season is progress. The key to further progression is to transfer our Ricoh form to the road.

Living in the south-west my mates follow Liverpool, Bristol City, Yeovil, Southampton and Sheffield United. None of them attend live matches unless it's a work freebie. And why? Are they newly-weds, playing football themselves, got too much work on? No. It's cheaper to watch the action on television and although I should despise their watching habits I can't really blame them. My cup final ticket cost £12 and that was a prime corner flag seat. A terrace ticket was a fiver. As we await a return to the showpiece occasion I have no idea how much a ticket would now cost. The thought is frightening.

Premiership days at Highfield Road would set you back £25

and more. Championship life is down a touch to £23. The cost of match day tickets nowadays alienates the families at near on £100 for the family of four. Fair weather fans will also baulk at the figure. Think about it, there's so much more you can do with that amount of money. If you're not that fussed about the team but going just because your mates are, you want something special for your hard-earned currency. I wouldn't pay more than the £26 I forked out to go to Southampton earlier this season. With petrol it's pushing £50. Throw in food, drink and the cost escalates further.

From the years 1993-96 my university mates follow Watford, Ipswich, Swindon and Charlton. Again, none of them attend for the reasons outlined above. They mock my support for City, who in their eyes are perennial strugglers. The one thing they have in common is at either 4.50pm or 9.30pm they associate Coventry with me. When our result comes up on Final Score the mocking valve triggers a response. They expect us to lose, simple as that.

Text messages fire across the country and I'm not slow to respond. They know we've had one glorious day, back in 1987. There were no mobile telephones then. I could only revel in the glory, yet deep down I was still pissed off with these people locally who had jumped on the bandwagon and pretended to follow my team. Not their team, my team.

For over two weeks prior to the Leeds game, sorting transport to the game proved much trickier than expected. With a lucky roster switch at work freeing up the day the only snag was freeing up the car. Train and coach networks were scoured but the Bristol-Coventry route proved to be totally inconvenient. Train via Gloucester and New Street or National Express coach via Birmingham. Each journey four hours long. My texts to Ade proved fruitless. Then came a divine vibration. Four days prior to the game I was able to plan for the weekend:

"Buy a ticket for the game, our plans have changed."
Heaven.

An instant text to dad to pick up a ticket for me, and Leeds at home was a definite. We travelled up en-masse. The journey had only just begun when the sight of a van embedded in the central reservation turned my stomach. Two years to the day I was hospitalised returning from a home draw with Gillingham, crushed between two lorries on the M42 and in hospital two weeks after the birth of my daughters. The day I was discharged some berk drove into the back of us as we left the hospital. I'm just about right now but driving to night matches is still not on. I don't trust anyone on the road, especially lorry drivers.

The services were dominated by Yeovil on their way to Huddersfield. No mean feat. One minibus' occupants bedecked in green and white replica shirts were not a day under sixty, and each one with a limp. Blackburn and Sunderland cars also prevalent, and this in Worcester. Dedication, or madness?

Coventry City Council has devised a clever ploy to position roadworks on every corner. Even more impressively they've taken the entry road to the Ricoh down to just one lane. At a time when we should be encouraging stayaway fans to return to the ground the barriers are thrown up to cause maximum disruption. This saw dad weaving in and out of his old stamping ground near Holbrooks to get us parked up with minimum fuss. Seats around us were empty as the teams took to the field. For the first time ever at a match I've attended, the PA asked people to take their seats as the bars on the concourse were rammed with minutes to go.

As King's Love and Pride blasted out, our row began to fill up and I look around at the cast of characters I'll be spending the next two hours with. First up a bloke who looks rough and half-cut, almost asleep. He's wearing the new City away kit which doubles as a display of what he's eaten this week. He stands up, alone, raises his arm like Superman and chants *"Come on City!"* He failed to reappear for the second half. Then came the group of five lads adamant we were in their seats. Read your tickets lads. Wrong row.

Finally, my pet hate. Mum, dad, son and girlfriend. The clock reads 3.15. Nescafe in hand. Absolutely no urgency whatsoever. They think they're at the theatre. Five minutes to half-time off they go back to the concourse for their half-time snacks. Returning minutes into the second half, they left the game with ten minutes left. What was the point?

As with last week's victory over Norwich the fans left in droves as the fourth official signalled three minutes to play. Let's work this one out. We're one up with minutes left. It's edge of the seat stuff. Leeds are pressing for the equaliser. Is it really time to go? You won't know the final score, for starters.

After so much doom and gloom at City over the years surely the team deserve an ovation at the final whistle. Why leave just so you can avoid the traffic? The journey home is part and parcel of the day out. A well-worked goal from Stern John, who now becomes our leading scorer with three, put paid to a poor Leeds side experiencing the traumas we faced upon relegation. Why does everyone hate Leeds United? Books could be written on the subject.

Turning on Radio 5 live as the lower league tables were read out the following unique statement was to be heard:

"The Championship has Cardiff and Birmingham top on 17 points, Burnley on 14, then Southampton, Preston and Coventry on 13."

I've never heard us in that breath before. Usually the bottom of the table is our forte.

Every season, 14 of the 92 teams secure promotion or Champions League places. A further 12 are relegated. That leaves 66 teams. Coventry have been part of those 66 ever since I started watching them. Aside from our greatest day all I have to show for my dedication and support is a solitary relegation. I've covered thousands of miles across the country as petrol has shot up in price over the years. We haven't had a top six finish in 35 years. My lifetime.

Chapter 6

Back to normal

"Rubbish performance. Utter rubbish!"
My brother used to be such an optimist. Always struggling to
find fault with City but at 26, realism has now dawned. Today he
paid £30 to watch a game of football. At least Dick Turpin wore
a mask, as the old joke goes. I've never paid more than £26 to
watch us play. Even in the Premiership we were never subject-
ed to downright robbery. Link this exorbitant fare with attend-
ing one of the worst-located grounds in the country and it
becomes a day of misery. When I say *"one of the worst-located
grounds in the country"* you know what's coming next. Yes, we
were away at Palace.

When I lived in South-East London, Selhurst was three stops
away on British Rail. Negotiating via the South Circular, I
wouldn't wish on anyone. Combined with our poor record there
it's no surprise our psyche maybe wasn't spot on. Away form can
be a major factor in a promotion campaign and a key denomina-
tor as to why we've never featured in one. Fortress Ricoh is all
well and good but one defeat at home and the pressure cranks
up. So why is our away form such an enigma?

The away following is loyal. And at least under Micky Adams
going a goal down isn't the end of the match. We sometimes fight
back and score. Yet the away-phobia remains. Are the overnight
stays too cushy? Perhaps it breeds a holiday culture? Away from
home in a nice hotel room with decent facilities, maybe too
relaxed? Is it all too comfortable?

Like my daughters, the players love their comfort blanket - the

Ricoh Arena. A superb venue with brand new, excellent, modern facilities. Running out at grotty Selhurst Park or tiny Portman Road is a huge letdown for them. We've been spoilt by our wonderful stage.

Or is it simply all in their heads? I ponder on this one after another single-goal defeat, our fourth of the season.

Another international break looms after Plymouth's visit. Ten games into the season will be an excellent benchmark to projecting our finish. A lack of vehicle custody prohibits my attendance and with dad in Spain and brother/step-brothers also absent we'll all be glued to Sky Sports News.

After 21 years in the top flight (in my supporting lifetime but 34 in total), simply assuming we'd always be there, life outside the top division has opened my eyes to the reality of modern football and its finances. It's not all about what happens on the pitch. Off the pitch decisions affect the playing side in a way I never experienced in the Premiership. If we wanted a player, we went out and bought him. You didn't give a thought to whether we could really afford him or not, we signed players when we needed. No-one questioned where the money came from.

Only when we'd tumbled off teletext page 303 and moved onto league table page 325 did financial murmurings begin to surface. Three months into our lower league tenure the club announced a £60 million debt. Chairman Bryan Richardson was ousted after his Premiership profligacy and director Mike McGinnity moved upstairs to fight the fire. ITV Digital then collapsed owing Football League clubs substantial revenue. We nearly folded.

My heart suddenly starts racing. Jeff Stelling interrupts Charlie Nicholas on the Sky Soccer Saturday panel to mention our terrific home record throughout the afternoon. It was the way his face contorted that left me in suspense. The vibe wasn't good.

Only minutes earlier I'd checked the table to see where a point would take us. More pessimism. With eight minutes to go we trailed. My initial reaction was to turn off the box but I couldn't. Dad needed the final score texted to Spain and Plymouth mate Kalvin in Washington relied on me to light up his weekend away with his wife.

The day had started so well. Up at the crack of dawn, it took nearly three hours to paint the garage a shade of sky blue. Once my ladies had departed with the car and various household stuff was completed I sat down for my first Soccer Saturday in nearly three years. Bolton and Liverpool served up mush to begin with but then Jeff and company entertained while I reclined for the duration of the afternoon.

Publication of the league table has seen us drop to 15th. The worry of relying on home form has come home to roost. I expected us to win today hands down. With ten games played you can evaluate the campaign so far:

We've lost half the games we have played.

Five defeats, all by a single goal.

Only eight goals have been scored.

15th position. Are we simply going to end up mid-table?

Four away defeats out of five which equals too much pressure on home fixtures.

Injury means Bischoff and Andrews are yet to play after joining this summer.

Virgo lasted a matter of minutes before injury potentially ended his season.

Tabb has played a handful of games due to injury.

Cameron today played his first full game – in the tenth match of the season.

Goal machines Kyle and McKenzie have one strike between them.

McNamee has suffered injury and suspension missing half the games so far.

There is a positive side, though:

Ward, Marshall and Birchall have played every game and excelled.

Hughes is back to his best form and Stern John has been superb.

The major problem we have now is the two-week international break. We need continuous games to sort the away form. Our next clump of fixtures see Southend and Wolves away, Colchester on Sky, Barnsley away then ending October with Birmingham visiting the Ricoh. In the negative zone I'm firmly entrenched at present we'll capitulate on a cold Friday night in Southend. The bigger opposition in Wolves may be more to our liking? Colchester are a side in form. Barnsley away on a cold Saturday is our usual banana skin. Remembering they turned us over in the Premiership I expect them to do it again. Then Blues at home with a full house. We need to stay unbeaten, build a run and be more resolute away from home.

Describing the post-relegation period as a struggle is a massive understatement. Four seasons of embarrassing reverses and ridiculously overpaid ex-Premiership players. Uncommitted performances, and 46 games instead of 38 to endure, adding to the agony. With the exception of Eric Black's brief reign, there hasn't been much to shout about. It's more been a case of shaking your head in complete disbelief. We've become victims of our own expectations, believing immediate promotion would be a case of turning up and putting on the shirt. That's why ongoing frustration lingers. The longer we have remained in this division, the lower the patience threshold.

It wasn't just me that was affected. Dad started to pick and choose his games, which was unheard of. Sometimes, with barely 200 visiting supporters the atmosphere has been nullified since our top-flight days. In the Premiership the visiting section of the Sky Blue stand was invariably sold out.

A goalless draw at home to Stockport drained his enthusiasm to the limit. That day, in his view, they were the better team. On a freezing November evening I squirmed through a display at home to Bradford on Bonfire Night that could have been the worst football match ever played. The journey home had no 606, just rockets and air bombs reverberating in the night sky for company. Farcical wasn't the word.

Pompey put four past us on a Wednesday night the season they swept all before them. I envied the euphoria and enjoyment of their massed ranks celebrating their dream season while we sat there with 'losing culture' etched on our foreheads. However, you have to remember that their fans had sat through years of lower division failure. The worm will turn at some point although the question on our lips, time and time again, is *"Can it get much worse?"* I should know by now that the answer is *"Yes."*

No stressful matchdays during the international break has seen me employ a new set of tactics last used in our first post-Premiership season; text updates that you pay for when no-one else can keep you informed. Teamtalk will transmit the bad news while I'm stuck on the bus returning home from work. Southend away on a cold, windswept evening is a Friday night experience, rare for us but a usual occurrence for our hosts. Back in the seventies teams like Stockport and Tranmere used to play regularly on Friday nights to attract support from their big city neighbours, but I can't imagine Southend get many surplus West Ham or Ipswich fans.

Sitting on the bus home the first vibration from my new gizmo gave me the team news. Very impressive; a 5-3-2 away formation smacks of a manager who knows where the problems lie and wants to make sure we don't let – ANOTHER – late goal in. By the time I was home twin bath time ensured that the mobile was switched on at half-time and I prepared for the vibrations.

Only one appeared:

"Southend 1 Coventry 1 (Hughes 41)".

So no opponent team goals get sent through? Or is because we live in a valley and the signal is woeful? I suppose I'll save the 25p per text fee if it only sends through our goals and it'll be a very cheap season. Leaving the phone in the kitchen while we cooked our tea the vibrations weren't happening. The longer the game goes on, the nearer the clock reaches 9.30pm, the more likely we'll let in a late one. After demolishing pilau rice and salmon pancakes a quick check of the handset saw two messages received. The first one, *"Southend 2 Coventry 2"*.

Hang on a minute. Who scored our second? The service is somewhat punctuated here. The worry is that I'll check the next message and we'll be 4-2 down. The turning point of the season is now upon us. The next text will either secure an away win or plunge us to yet another reverse. It's now 9.27. Any strike now will be decisive. *"Adebola 79"* is all I need to read. 3-2 up. Can we hang on for a much needed three away points? Suddenly, it vibrates again!

The stomach turns as I open the text:

"Any score?"

Christ! It's Rich texting from Spain. A quick flick onto Sky Sports News confirms our victory and the call to Spain is a pleasurable one. All of a sudden everything is rosy. The thought of work tomorrow isn't so bad after all and we're up to ninth place, two points off second. Enjoy the moment. Ade is stunned by the victory. *"Jesus Christ, I've just gone off like a faulty firework!"*

The erratic nature of either the service or our location then sees the half-time score sent through to me. But it was money well spent today; the change in fortune is characterised by a deflected strike, stonewall penalty and a very fortuitous rebound which sent us to victory. Lady Luck is on our side. Finally.

Three goals is a real bonus, especially away from the fortress. There's no way at 25p per text I'm continuing with updates when I can get them free most of the time. Superstition doesn't play a part here, economics do. Southend mate Ricki predicted the result before the game: *"I have watched enough games already this season to know we are going down, I think you will win tomorrow."*

Chapter 7

Struggles continue on the road

January 2005. Newly-appointed chief firefighter Micky Adams pulled us back from the brink of near-relegation that was the legacy of Peter Reid's disastrous six-month tenure and the knock-on from previous tenants Strachan, Nilsson and McAllister. McGinnity departed mid-season due to failing health. Labour MP Geoffrey Robinson stepped into the breach. It's no wonder McGinnity's health failed, having tried manfully to fight the £60 million debt incurred by the previous regime.

Back to the present and a sixth defeat in 12 games arrives courtesy of Wolves away. Maybe it's a self-belief thing (i.e. we haven't got any as soon as we lose sight of the Ricoh). Chasing a goal deficit with seventy minutes left I was tempted to turn off Sky Sports. One of these days I'll turn it back on later in the evening and get a nice surprise. That's never happened because I've never done it. Mid-table now, the heady heights of sixth place are forgotten. In *Staying Up* by Rick Gekoski, Gordon Strachan marks the season's final position by the 12th fixture. If that's the case for us then plenty of home wins will balance out the away defeats.

Our billing on Sky has now dropped to having no goal flash reporter at our games. The final score appeared at the bottom of the live goal updates. We didn't receive one mention during the second half. Forgotten in media eyes, our profile is continually lowered. Cardiff lead the division by six clear points.

There's an acceptance, an admission, a time-honoured belief that we never retrieve deficits in games. Rarely. Hardly. Ever.

We play live again on Sky next week with newly-promoted Colchester the visitors. The club has kindly offered me two free tickets.

Worried that the attendance will be the lowest this season the marketing department has gone into overdrive and attempted to entice people into the ground. I'll be there alright, in the Walkabout bar two doors down from my office and ideal as I finish work at 7.30. The three other Bristol Sky Blues will join me and see how many other closet Sky Blue fans erupt every time we score. By the time the game is played the weekend's fixtures will have shunted us further down the league to increase the pressure only slightly, but highlighting the importance of a 'must win' conclusion.

With our weak link full-backs now out of contention through injury part of me sighs with relief. The rest wonders who the hell will fill the gaps? Since relegation City have been occasionally brilliant and sometimes woeful exponents of the loan system. Due to our financial 'oversights' in Premiership times the word borrowing rears its little head. Not in financial overtures, just in loaning players from Premiership clubs. Players either recovering from injury, dropped and discarded or shop window material. Each with their own criteria and certainly without the club's interests at heart. They don't care whether City pick up and do well as they're only in the loan for themselves.

At one point under Gary Mac a home game against West Ham saw no fewer than five loanees fielded. Obvious successes include Richie Partridge and Luke Steele, plus Craig Hignett for a few brief weeks. They all contributed quality to our not-good-enough team. Many others proved to be either past their best, unfit or uncaring.

Only now in our sixth season since the drop do we have no loan signings. All our squad are now brought in on contracts. It seems the beg, steal and borrow days are a thing of the past. I hope.

Along with Robinson came inspiration in the shape of the Big

Three, a new management committee led by managing director Paul Fletcher. With inspiration on the pitch from Dennis Wise and the creative cameos of Don Hutchison, 2005-06 ended in eighth position. The best finish since relegation, it raised expectations to previously untold levels.

Walkabout was vacant. It was a far cry from the Sunday afternoon 4.00 viewing when there's not a spare seat in the house. The pull down screen firmly pulled up, it was flat screen for us, viewed sat at the tables usually reserved for swaying into the early hours. The happy hour burger and chips were well received, as was lemonade and lime for the driver, Carling and Tooheys for the Bristol Sky Blues. As the elite City eleven appear on the screen, the once weak and now vacant full-back slots were solidly filled with loan stars. So all the money spent in the summer, all the players brought in and we can't field a decent left or right back?

Micky, obviously not too proud to beg and borrow, loaned Richard Duffy for the third successive season from Portsmouth. Why the hell doesn't he sign permanently? He'll never get a place in their team and we can guarantee regular action. Clive Clarke from Sunderland filled the left-back slot and it was looking better already.

With Sky Blue shirts anonymous by their absence and certainly no Colchester hardcore present the banter flowed as City moved into a two goal lead. Volume was at a premium as music took precedence, the atmosphere resembling the Ricoh with plenty of wide open spaces. Only 16,178 attended, the lowest of the campaign so far. The marketing campaign was obviously flawed.

Suddenly the banter stopped. Five minutes remaining and Colchester pull a goal back. Immediately the flowing conversation was muted as the table was pounded by nervous fists. The four extra minutes took an eternity until loud roars took over the pub as the final whistle sounded. Up to tenth.

With the season a full on yo-yo, winning away at Barnsley on

Saturday will be massive, with the top six in sight. Calm that optimistic bloke down! The downpour that greeted the victorious quartet on leaving Walkabout couldn't dampen the smiles. Seeing the goals when I got home showed just how good they were, even if the game wasn't a classic.

Living in South Gloucestershire I'm as close to the club now as I've ever been. The accent is still there; you can't take the Coventry out of me. I talk about the club to others but more to defend them, to justify their failings. I stick up for them even in defeat. I end up getting defensive when the team are slated. Fighting back when the latest defeat hails us a laughing stock. Deep down, I'm a realist. We've not been good enough and the spell in the lower division has been far too long. We shouldn't be here. When you suffer relegation you expect to bounce straight back, every supporter believes a spell in the lower division will be brief. But when the reality hits home that it's a long-term stay not a holiday, it hurts.

Top assets are sold on with cheap impersonators brought in. Players not good enough to avoid the drop are still being paid wages that will cripple the club once the parachute payments cease. With no guarantee of an immediate return the clubs cover their backs as they struggle to adapt to the quicker pace outside the top tier. There hasn't been much to shout about with unfashionable Coventry City. Back in 1980, aged six, it was all so different. We were going to win the league back then.

"You don't know what you're doing!" That's what rang out from the City following at Barnsley. The reason? Micky subbed Leon McKenzie instead of Kevin Kyle or Dele Adebola. The substitute making his debut for us, Wayne Andrews, ignored the fuss completely. Using his first touch to cut inside his second saw him fire superbly into the far corner. Obviously Micky did know what he was doing after all. Back to back wins; priceless.

The third away win of the season catapults us into eighth place and suddenly football is a wonderful creation. But there's still a nagging problem, thanks to the criticism levelled at Adams after the terrific job he's done. Why are we slating our chief firefighter? This goes back to the expectation levels after relegation and the hype generated by Operation Premiership. Yes, we should expect to beat teams like Barnsley. However, sometimes it doesn't go to plan. Our manager gambled with a substitution and it worked. To effect change within sixty seconds of stepping onto the pitch is something he may never ever effect again. The loyal following behind the goal at Oakwell will have cheered their socks off when Andrews netted. The cheers will have interrupted their own jeers. That's football supporters for you, and I'm as bad as anyone.

The late strike robbed me of a £20 payout. For the first time ever I waged a bet on City not winning. Why? I suppose if we drew I'm compensated. A draw gives me the evening's Chinese takeaway. I only bet on the draw at 9/4 compared to the defeat at 7/4. Not too much difference but I could feel the guilt at the thought of betting on us to lose. I figured a win or draw and I'll be happy. I convinced myself I was only increasing my chances of being in a good mood on Saturday evening.

My earliest recollection of Highfield Road is Crystal Palace striker Clive Allen's look of disbelief as play is waved on after his shot rebounded back off the net stanchion. The Coventry team played to the whistle and pretended it had never happened. It was so obviously a goal; even aged six it was clear to me and everyone around us. I saw it go in. It hit the back of the net. In 1980 there was no video technology available to the referee and in 2007 we are still debating the same issue

"Coventry and West Brom will be up there at the end of the season and this is a massive win for us."

The above were the post-match comments from Birmingham full-back Stephen Kelly. I've never heard anyone describe beating us as a massive win or that we're promotion contenders. The highest league crowd I've been in at a home game saw Birmingham inflict the first defeat I've witnessed at the Ricoh, at the sixteenth attempt. 27,212!!! Ade gunned the time machine down the outside lane and the approach to the ground was reached in just over an hour and twenty. Tickets were collected just before kick-off to see us then confronted by the largest queues ever to get into a City game. Usually people are streaming out.

The club still can't plan for large crowds. With five minutes to kick-off the cash turnstile was opened up and we streamed in. For a further twenty minutes fans continued to file in, the away masses delayed by a crash on the M6.With their allocation nearly sold out they added to the atmosphere in vast numbers.

Our seats were right by the corner flag at player's-eye level. I now know why I prefer sitting higher up but when the tickets are bought by others you can't grumble. One thing it does accentuate is the sheer pace the game is played at. Endurance training seems pointless as the game is played in such short, sharp bursts with the emphasis on explosive power. With the rush to get in the bladder was neglected and the half-time scrum down for the khazi ridiculous, especially given the size of the crowd. Do we have enough loos? When the ground was designed did they honestly believe we would attract crowds this high? For a split second I wished we were crap again with meagre attendances and no queues anywhere. At present we're queuing to get to the ground, through the turnstile, for the gents and then to get out. Our £3 car park fee tonight reflects the fact that you have further to walk to the ground. For a fiver you can knock ten minutes off your walk.

Chasing a one goal deficit City gave it their all but couldn't knock down the Blue defensive door.

The whistle blows to inflict our seventh defeat of the season. With no game until Monday, when our visit to Stoke will be televised, the opportunity arises for everyone below us to again win their weekend game and increase the pressure on us to get a result to spring back into the top half. The pendulum is swinging between top and bottom half, win and defeat. No medium ground has been attained as yet. A few draws might stabilise us and hopefully allow us to retrieve a game from the jaws of defeat.

Tonight we've succumbed to yet another single goal defeat, our sixth 1-0 of the campaign. It must all be in their heads. Soon it will become a burden or has it already? Can a deficit be retrieved or do we have to lead a game to stand a chance of victory?

Amusing chant of the night: *"Shit on the Villa"* rang out from both ends of the ground. Blues have a deep-rooted hatred that can only come from spending a century in the shadows of a bigger team and by all accounts it's returned with interest. We pretend Villa are our deadly rivals, but deep down we know they're not fussed. I got home at midnight in time to watch the goal again.

Chapter 8

Back to the eighties

The West Ham v Arsenal cup final of 1980 saw me dutifully filling in the Match magazine pullout as the game progressed. FA Cup finals, similar to the Natwest Trophy cricket final, were a day-long extravaganza. Coverage began at nine with Des Lynam guiding you through the events preceding kick-off. It was an event in itself prior to the money men dictating the format of the showpiece event in years to come.

On ordinary Saturdays, from 4.40 onwards Grandstand's vidiprinter gave you the goals as they happened. James Alexander Gordon read out the bad news at the classified check on Sports Report. The tone of his voice ensured you knew instantly how your team had fared. Back in the early eighties and into the nineties there was no Jeff Stelling and the panel with coverage from midday. No three-hour Soccer AM every Saturday morning. Star Soccer on Sunday afternoons presented half an hour of division one action with the legendary commentary of Hugh Johns. We rarely featured. Live football was a real treat, very much an exception and not the rule. Following the live scores on the internet or your mobile phone was light years away. Teletext only appeared through the night on BBC2.

The weather was freezing, fog blanketing the country. Walkabout had the roof on and provided the offering for Sky's fourth City feature already this season. Burgers and chips were again consumed and the Bristol Sky Blue contingent down to two. The venue was deserted, a far cry from the previous day's Premiership action. You can't move in there come four on a

Sunday, even for Wigan v Bolton. Premiership clashes pack the place to the rafters, the Championship is a sideshow.

My negative mindset saw me wage £3 on the draw, my logic that surely we will finish all square at some point this year. It literally was a tale of mist (sorry!) chances, the majority by Stoke during a period that had me praying for blanket fog cover and an abandonment. At pitch level it was fine but from five yards away on the box too many players were hiding in both senses of the word.

After conceding to the kind of top corner finish you used to draw on paper at school, I should have left. Of course, I didn't. The misery was endured, the gnawing knowledge that yet another single goal defeat was forthcoming. Player and fan mentality is such that we could have all left and gone home and not affected the outcome. When we score first, we win. Simple. Surely? An easy problem to solve and one familiar with City teams down the years. Slowly but surely the club is becoming far too reactive. Substitutions are only made to react to changes in the scoreline. Why not change the course of the game before the opposition do? I'm surely not the only one to think this? We left in silence, walking past a gaggle of Stoke at the bar.

The cold walk to the car and the foggy drive home cheered me up no end. True to form, I still watched the goal when I got home. With nothing you can do about a strike like that it really is a shame we use it as an excuse to mirror the crapness.

In 1980, outside the football world, The Empire Strikes Back was top on the big screen. Shortly before Christmas John Lennon was shot dead outside his New York home. Philips invented the compact disc and roller blades made their entrance on UK streets. Top loading video recorders and Grifter bikes were resident in every household.

My relationship with the club has lasted 27 years and counting. The only person I've known for longer is my dad. Over the years we've watched City with my brother Rich. We're still here all those years on, unlike the many who dropped off the cup run bandwagon when the fun stopped. University years in London enabled me to watch City in the capital over a three-year period. I was unfaithful on a number of occasions, taking in QPR and Leyton Orient fixtures. At £10 a visit QPR was an attractive student hangout. They entertained with Ferdinand and Sinclair up front, Wilkins pulling the strings in midfield. Watching as a neutral I sat with a smug grin. Witnessing other supporters going through the emotions was a pleasant change from my normal match day experience. I fought through the underground traffic then watched the match and caught the tube home. City's result that day was still the priority in my mind.

***

Tactic: the manoeuvre used to achieve a particular aim or task.

Proactive: to effect change.

Reactive: to react to change.

Derby manager Billy Davies' triple substitution on the hour swung things their way. Two weeks previously Micky Adams' tactical switch won the game at Barnsley. Today, like so often this season, we waited until the damage was done and reacted to the proactive nature of the opposition manager.

It didn't begin well. Being asked to sit down by the miserable old guy sat behind me I could take. What I couldn't accept was the fact that it was 2.55 and the game hadn't started. His complaint: his two sons couldn't see the dance troupe performing on the pitch. My reply: go and sit in the Junior Sky Blues section like I will when my daughters want to attend. 19,701 turned up today and 3,000 of those travelled from the East Midlands. There were no queues to get in; even taking a pee was a breeze.

The 2-1 defeat leaves us in 15th position in an incredibly tight division. Nine losses already out of 17 games isn't great. If six of those defeats had been draws I wouldn't be sitting here whining and repeating myself. It's important to put it in perspective: it's no different to other seasons. In seasons to come the familiar pattern will be repeated time and time again. After last season's eighth place finish optimism has perhaps gone a bit daft, especially in my head.

The loss of Wise and now McSheffrey is hitting us way harder than I ever imagined. Captain Hughes was demoted prior to kick off and subsequently dropped from the squad, a personality clash with the manager the much-vaunted rumour doing the rounds. My guess is that he won't figure again while Adams is in charge.

Our side contains no set piece specialist. Free kicks on the edge of the opposition's box rarely trouble the keeper; I can't remember the last time we scored direct from a free kick, or a corner. We should be working on these weaknesses in training.

Back in 1994 part of my Sports Science degree coursework involved three weeks observation of the Sky Blues training and coaching methods. Interesting, and not once did the players work on their weaknesses. These guys are paid thousands of pounds a week to play football. Spending time working on technique and skills seems little to ask.

Anyway, this season is getting me down. I expected much more. What I'm getting is less than a goal a game from a team with a mental block away from home. Our home venue is no longer a fortress, more like a ruined castle with the drawbridge down and the moat drained. My mates have given up on the piss taking. Texts are few and far between. Even they accept how poor we are.

* * *

Panini sticker albums came and went at 6p a pack. I failed to complete a solitary one. Shiny badges always carried greater swap potential, you could get three players for a badge - five if the players were Scottish. Later, Saint and Greavsie entertained us prior to kick off while I ate burger and oven chips to soak up the previous night's Fosters down the Silver Sword. Gabriel Clarke did the roving reports and Elton Welsby presented the Big Match Live. Sportsnight was the BBC's midweek Match of the Day, showing highlights of internationals and European ties. No league games were televised until 1983 when Spurs and Forest lit the live touch paper.

Chapter 9

Wednesday sunk on a Saturday

An evening wedding reception in deepest, darkest Somerset put paid to a second successive visit to the Ricoh. Instead I had the company of Sky Sports Soccer Saturday and text updates from dad to ensure I really was there. The afternoon's events panned out as follows:

"One down against ten men direct from owls corner. Equalised straight away from own goal."

Followed in close succession by *"Wednesday down to nine men"*. We'll struggle to break them down now. Honestly. Don't think we haven't messed it up before in this position. Forest at home in the first season post-relegation springs immediately to mind.

Pure unexpected elation vibrated in rapid succession with: *"McKenzie follow up for City 50"* and *"McKenzie again 55"*. Rich responded to my 4-0 premonition with a bet on the draw at half-time and Wednesday winning 2-1 at the finish.

As it transpires two red cards, an own goal and a goal direct from a corner ensured the action was frenetic. Even at half time with the Owls down to nine men the ingrained Cityness in me expected the visitors to hold on or even sneak a win. The interval change into my suit for our evening out proved a lucky charm but there's no way I'm dressing up each match to ensure we take the points. What it did provoke was slightly worrying for me even if we are now 11th, the play-offs only four points away.

One of my daughters freaked at the sight of me in something other than jeans and Stan Smiths. Doesn't she realise I don't really want to dress up or go to work at 6am each day? A suit is not for me, I'd much rather write for a living. Once this had been overcome with gentle coaxing and cuddles we had to leave with us 3-1 up. I was fairly confident we could hang on to our lead when we left the house with half an hour remaining. No further vibrations from my mobile ensured that the lack of Five Live action due to my daughters' nursery rhymes monopolising the airwaves enabled me to finally relax during a game with such a comfort zone.

After last season's fixture two Wednesday fans died returning home on the M69. Their accident has made me realise again how fortunate I was to survive mine. Both sets of fans sang Hi Ho Silver Lining as a tribute before kick-off, which was extremely well respected. A nice touch.

After our first win in four games I'm buzzing again. The wonderful game of football is such a teaser of emotions. I hadn't even thought what would happen if we did lose today; my Coventrian mindset didn't even look at the table to see where victory could raise us. My only concern was how far we could drop.

Turning 18 on the day Andre Agassi first triumphed at Wimbledon coincided with the arrival of Sky Digital. It was a big *"Hello!"* to the Premier League and pound signs abounded. Our neighbours, the only family in the street with a dish, invited us over for Monday night football.

We were envious but no amount of washing up and running round with the hoover could persuade the wage earner to cough up the fee. How times have changed; now he's even got Sky Plus. Ian Darke and Andy Gray have taken football commentary to a new level while new technology, Playercam and Fanzone provide unheard-of additions.

A tentative *"Did you go, Mr Jinx?"* to Ade who has yet to see us win this season drew an immediate reply:

"I can't believe it, I saw a victory, we played really well."

I was also staggered. Two wins on the bounce and we're back

in business. A pre-match traffic jam saw the City squad catch the Central Line to White City, mingling with Fulham and Hammers fans en route. As Micky quite rightly stated afterwards, preparation is nonsense. City just walked out of White City tube station and past the Springbok pub to Loftus Road. They then went out and secured their third 1-0 away success.

I write this at 9pm on the Sunday evening. Due to the TV rights scenario I have to wait for the Football League Review on Sky at midnight to watch Adebola's winning strike. If we'd lost I'd be tuned into 401 for the Ashes final day but that can wait. I have a winning goal to view and only then can I watch England attempt to stave off defeat in the first test at Brisbane.

The season has a fascinating symmetry at present:

P19 W9 D1 L9 F19 A19 P28

We're in ninth place, nine points off top spot and nine points off the relegation zone. Six clean sheets and eight single-goal defeats highlight the inconsistent first three months, which have mirrored my emotions; up and down, can be bothered, can't be bothered, I don't care. Yet I love it.

Up next is Preston away, where we've lost our last five fixtures. The first season post-relegation saw Rich and I travel up by club coach. Never again. A 4-0 defeat was the game that saw a City fan run onto the pitch to confront Nilsson and Hedman. The sheer frustration of life in the Football League got to him and he vented what we were all feeling. It was an awful day and summed up the situation, post-Premiership.

The early eighties brought hooliganism to my naïve and young impressionable eyes. Leeds kindly removed our brown away seats after we trounced them 4-0 in 1980-81. Pockets of brawling with Leicester in 1983 and bricks raining in as we left the ground in 1985 courtesy of West Ham followers. Fights would erupt on a regular basis as away supporters sat wherever they liked. It became the norm to look across the stadium and see clusters of yellow-jacketed police and stewards moving in to quell the disturbances. At times it would distract from the action on the pitch.

On one occasion we watched two of our own fighting after one bellowed 'advice' to Sean Flynn. Flynn was a real grafter with a prodigious leap and didn't take kindly to our friend shouting out during a break in play that he was useless. The other one told him to pack it in. Suddenly a fist flew past my right ear to connect with the guy sat to the right of me. Even funnier was the sight of the same pair hugging as Flynn immediately set up Dion Dublin for the winning goal.

Chapter 10

Fortune favours the brave

For the armchair internet viewer there was the delight of reading **Preston 1 Coventry 1 Adebola 80**. This was all happening while Gordon Ramsay was dishing out the expletives on Kitchen Nightmares. The ensuing glee can only be understood if you support an unfashionable and inconsistent lower league team.

Not believing for one moment that it would actually happen, it caught me right on my heels. The loss of custody of the Sky remote brought about the introduction of the laptop. Being a natural defeatist I instinctively thought why bother to log in because we'll only lose 1-0. The optimist in me thought log in and something unbelievably unSky Blue will happen. The form has got to change sometime. And it did. The greed in me then expected us to win. We're never happy.

The point still raised Preston to the summit while we dropped to eleventh. The fact we've never won at Deepdale totally influenced my thoughts of leaving the Toshiba in the case. Fortune favours the brave, or insane. You just have to follow your team's fortunes during the course of a match. It isn't fair to the team to let them down and leave them be. You owe them the support even though you've no control over anything that happens out on that pitch.

As I bounded out the door to work at 6.50 the following morning the difference an avoidance of defeat makes to your state of mind is massive. Wide awake for a change, the hour-long journey enjoyed rather than abhorred. This could well be a turning point as we approach the festive period.

Micky Quinn was always visible. Especially in my local book-ies in Cheylesmore. As an A level student with too much spare time on his hands the William Hill shop down Daventry Road was an attractive option, a place where I could actually earn some money. Ten one pound bets during the afternoon card; hardly big league. Micky Quinn knew everyone. Other players would be with him and also by his side in the Pink Parrot night-club. Back in the early nineties supporters didn't go running to the local press or radio station as they do today. He scored goals, was great with the fans and mixed with everyone. From November onwards he scored a lot of goals over a short period of time. The highlight was a double against title-chasing Villa on Boxing Day. So long as he did it on the pitch who cared what he did off it? Seeing the players out and about made them go up even further in our admiration.

While away in Australia during 1998, Soccer Weekly kept me in the loop. The previous season Dion Dublin topped the Premier League goals list. There's pride when one of your own is up there challenging for the Golden Boot, especially if you're one of the smaller clubs. He makes the top scorers table in the newspapers and has you hoping he'll notch again to receive extra coverage. The downside to this is speculation, which turns into transfer rumours. Before you know it your key asset has been cashed in.

Our leading lights in recent years have struggled to top 15 goals out of 46 games. When I returned in December 1998 we staved off relegation, for a change. I knew it would be a difficult season when I sat up until 3am, in Sydney, listening to Five Live on the World Service and hearing James Alexander Gordon's immortal words, *"Coventry City 1 Newcastle United 5."*

Christmas shopping may play some part in the sub-20,000 crowd today. A rare four-match unbeaten run is unheard of for our inconsistent bunch. Isn't it only the top teams who go twen-ty-odd matches without defeat? We've hit eight or nine in the past and to really stamp our mark on the division a long run is needed to emphasise whatever promotion credentials we may be harbouring.

Dad, Adam and I reached the seats with ample time to spare. The concourse bars were a hive of activity and consequently the gents a queuing procession. The afternoon began well. By 3.00 both sides and officials had no-showed. No sign of anyone. When our heroes and Stoke finally appeared, the toss was conducted quicker than a Ronaldo shuffle and this threw the tannoy announcer. He proceeded to welcome new loan signing Clive Clarke to the Ricoh. Clarke, with us now for six weeks, happened to be standing next to new loan signing Darren Currie.

If I was announcing the teams to the crowd the clipboard would be cast aside. Not wanting to sound big-headed but I'd do it from memory. Five Live ensures its commentary teams learn the names of the players in front of them for that very reason. That's why they work for the BBC and not at Coventry City where usual MC legend Stuart Linnell was conspicuous by his absence.

A quick observation of the crowd surrounding us again highlighted the reason we sit somewhere different each game. We never used to move around at Highfield Road. Sat in the same seat for years, the people around us were pretty normal. This was the Main Stand after all. Today, to the right and sat in the row in front is an angry young man. He has an opinion about every decision, backed up by leaping out of his seat in each instance to front the away support from a safe distance of over 100 yards. A brave lad he's not. He stands up right at the point when Adebola hits the post. This guy's anticipation is superb but obscures mine.

He's unaware the bars are only open before the game and close after half-time. You can see the crowd stifle a smirk as he mentions out loud he's off for a beer at the start of the second half. He returns swiftly. Fortunately for everyone around him he then leaves with the five minutes of added time just displayed to the crowd. His cronies leave with him, no doubt influenced by his decision.

Sat behind is the equivalent of Mr Commentary. Highly amusing, with a not too annoying voice, his observations are spot on. However, it would do my head in if I sat by him every game, although not as much as sitting by the Angry Young Man. If only he could see how embarrassing his actions are, and in time he will. We've all been there and behaved like that. The game finished goalless, by the way. Mid-table is becoming our niche.

In the eighties football matches finished at 4.40. The BBC1 vidiprinter would be flickering through the bad news as I sat glued to the moving cursor. There was no colour-coded team names to indicate which team had scored. As we moved into the nineties Sky's monopoly increased half-time from 10 to 15 minutes. The subsequent addition in recent seasons of added time ensured that 4.50 is the earliest you can expect to get away, and today it's 5pm on the nose. More value for your money, I suppose it could be argued.

Wherever you are in the world, when your team is playing, you just have to know the score. You must follow the outcome of the whole game. Why listen to part then go off and do something else? In a different timezone you can't sleep until the final whistle. Almost predictably, it's a defeat. Why stay up until three in the morning for Manchester United away? There's no way you're not going to find out that result. You just have to know.

You can only move on once the final whistle blows. Then you're pissed off and your day's been ruined. As soon as the live Sky game finishes your wife grabs the remote to change the channel. Hang on! What about the post-match reaction? What about the goal that wasn't? Get your hands off the remote and let me watch the end of the programme. Please don't ask me to do something now. I'm fed up. Her thought is that when a film ends the credits roll. With football, seeing us lose is not enough. I need to be told why we lost. The full-time whistle merely suspends the concluded drama. It still needs to be analysed and I need to see the goals again. I can't influence the result, I just need to know who to blame.

This gets worse as you age. The more experienced you are, so more of an analytical position is adopted. In my younger years it was straight onto the next game. Now I can see it all so much clearer. Of course I could have done better.

***

I missed one of the highlights of the football season; the FA Cup Third Round draw. This used to be heard, not seen, Monday lunchtime, 12.30, on Radio 2. Now it's anybody's guess as to where and when the balls will be twirled. Ex-cup winners, managers, legends and officials are chosen to make the draw. Of course when the dream tie, the non-league collection of postmen, plumbers and plasterers is drawn at home to Chelsea comes up, the tie is switched on police advice. The romance of the competition sucked out in a move that benefits financially but removes the threat of any kind of upset. Back in 1989 there was no such option to our opponents in the third round, Sutton United. The non-leaguers unceremoniously dumped us out before falling 8-0 to Norwich in the next round. However, we are not a big club. The minnows fancy their chances against us. If you move back through the years we've been easy pickings for numerous sides. It's only the elite whiners that get their way and massively reduce the chance of any banana skin.

Now drawn on Sky with an official from the FA making sure there's no cheating, the 3.15 draw was tricky knowing we had friends round. Once they had left it was straight onto Skytext and into the Championship section. As the initial highlights of the draw excluded us I concluded that there was no Premiership defeat away from home on the horizon. Moving through the thirty-two ties past page 1/4 there was no sign of us. Tentatively onto page 2/4, again no sign. I also noticed Bristol City and Rovers were yet to appear. And then the moment arrived. No need to flick through the draw any further. **Bristol C v Coventry**. Yessssssssssssssssssssssssssssssssssssssssssssssss!!!!!!

I've lived down here just over ten years and aside from Saints away this is the nearest game in all that time. The texts started flying across the network. Not from the sole Bristol City fan at work but from fellow Sky Blues delighted at finally getting a City game on our doorstep. Then came the slight snag. I knew I was down to work that weekend. With the travel industry the chaotic season is January and February. I tried to play it posi- tively but the realist in me was thinking "*Shite! I've got no chance.*" Then came the Get Out of Jail Free and Attend the Football card. A swap, with the relief on a par with finding out I had the day off to get married.

Then came another snag. For the first time in many years both Bristol sides have made it to the FA Cup third round draw. Rovers replay at Bournemouth and the outcome will determine whether it's a Saturday or Sunday. They win but fortunately, making life easier for me, their tie at home to Hereford is a Friday night affair and we get centre stage on Saturday. Traditional FA Cup footy on third round day. Guaranteed to be freezing cold, raining and kicking off at three o'clock. We were never likely to feature on a live schedule on cup weekend so the thought of driving half an hour into Bristol compared to 100 miles to the Ricoh is going to be savoured. We should fill our allocation comfortably and stuff them. That would make me very happy.

It's also twenty years since we won the cup. The quarter-final is the furthest we've reached since that wonderful day. Can we put a run together, get a few lucky draws and avoid the big guns?

Trends catch on in football. Dad was embarrassed to previ- ously-unattainable levels thanks to the only inflatable banana ever seen in the Main Stand at Highfield Road. It was so large I struggled to see the game, let alone the people sat behind me. I did pretend to be cool but looking back it must have looked a bit daft. It failed to reappear after its debut as I decided to leave it behind. This followed the range of inflatable objects seen around the grounds in the late eighties. Haddocks, hammers, dolls, beach balls. Cup runs saw the inflatable range multiply in numbers. Where they all came from, and where they ended up, no-one knows.

Chapter 11
Even the bogey sides are being beaten

Burnley at the Ricoh was one game I could miss. Being paid to work that day played a major part in my non-attendance of a fixture against one of our bogey sides. Our half-time lead was one I expected. The old expectation levels are returning but the second half dragged along, visualising the league table and flicking between the teletext pages. You're glued to the screen awaiting the buzz when your team suddenly appears on the screen. Most likely it's the stomach-wrenching feeling when you go one down, but we hung on for a fifth match unbeaten and top half karma maintained.

The halfway point of the campaign is nearly upon us. This season has been so much better than last year but at times it's felt worse. The same old inconsistency, with a lack of goals inherent. Right now our defence is impenetrable and this previous weakness led to our lower half residence over the last five seasons. The problems start when the defence has an off-day.

We suffered for years in the Highfield Road Main Stand. Whenever the Mexican wave approached it fragmented dramatically. I used to cringe as it snaked around the ground towards us. Once it moved into the directors box adjacent, it was limping then picked up pace and flew around the stadium, away fans included. I used to cringe whenever the West Terrace chanted, *"Main Stand, Main Stand give us a song."* You just knew there'd be either no response or, worse, one lunatic would strike up a solo chant. He was either on secondment from another area of the ground or had sampled the local hostelries prior to kick-off.

Never did we see so many Mexican waves than the season that has gone down in folklore: 1986-87.

Nine days on I still can't bring myself to watch the five goals West Brom stuck in our net. I still haven't read a match report. Wired up to Talksport the writing was on the wall after only half a minute. At half-time I was praying my battery would die on me.

The humiliation continued to be followed by mates crawling out of the Slate Coventry woodwork. Texts rained in. Manc Tony on his return from Manchester, City of Misery:

"What happened to the mighty cov - think promotion has been kissed goodbye!"

I thought that weeks ago. The end of the mighty five game unbeaten run sees us slide to 14th. It's yet another negative with the only positive being that if we lose at Luton next week we can't drop any further. The fact that Sunderland, rock bottom after losing the first five games, are now above us further enhances my negative body language.

Over the years I've put in so much more supporting City than I've received back. There have been moments to savour because it's not been last-day survival every season. When the team produce a collective reward for the fans like they did in 1987, it makes it all worthwhile.

John Sillett and George Curtis introduced fun and flair to our Saturday afternoons. With the impregnable Oggy lined up alongside skipper Brian Kilcline, Lloyd McGrath and Michael Gynn grafted in the engine room, Cyrille Regis led from the front with the supporting role played by Dave Bennett. Legends.

P23 W10 D3 L10 F21 A 23 P33

So far so good at halfway. This season has certainly been better than last. Only Southend have scored less goals but with us four points off the play-offs and twelve off relegation (the normal over the shoulder thought) the only way is up. I hope.

Twelve new players have been brought in since the end of last season. At the present time only four are regulars. The heartbeat of the team contains five of last season's cast while four loan acquisitions are now present in the team. Of the 12 arrivals eight have played only a handful of games and our top scorer has five. The above facts and figures smack of mid-table instability. City are as inconsistent as usual, brilliant one minute, you know what's going to happen the next. I'm as expectant as ever but the pre-season hype has yet to be justified.

At 12-years-old it was exciting stuff to watch. We were winning for a change and the defeats became less frequent. It was great to be on page one of the teletext league tables. We were seen and were making an impression. January 1987 was absolutely freezing. City drew Bolton at home on a tricky, icy pitch. FA Cup third round day. Three first half goals put paid to a Bolton side then in the old division three. Monday's lunchtime draw saw us pitted away to Manchester United. Unbelievably, Keith Houchen, signed from Hartlepool, scrambled in a first half winner to send our hopes and optimism rocketing skywards.

I'm sat on the pan close to half-time. Suddenly Jeff Stelling's dulcet tones break the bad news as so often he does. However, my £1 wager on Luton to lead at half-time then City to triumph by the end saw the odds of 33/1 perk up my demeanour. Driving in the car for the majority of the second half, my clenched fist celebrated our equaliser on the hour. And my elation was muted sharply when a quickfire brace saw my bet go up in smoke. Final Score yet again confirmed the worst. I couldn't face teletext or Sky. A key period of three games in six days will either rocket us back towards the play-offs or cement us as has-beens for yet another season.

Round Five sent us to soaring division two side Stoke City. 8,000 visitors packed in behind the goal at the old Victoria Ground. My mate Lee, his dad Alan, and I were sat on the front row of the stand above the terrace. Micky Gynn's carefully slotted effort right into the corner where we were sat took us into the quarter-finals. Next up we were away at Hillsborough against Howard Wilkinson's superfit Sheffield Wednesday. Up the M1 we followed the mass of sky blue en route to Sheffield. 15,000 fans made the journey this time. Front row seats again in the upper section of the Leppings Lane End gave us the view of Wednesday's fantastic Kop terrace. 54,000, the largest attendance I had ever been part of.

The pitch looked so wide, square even. The emphatic roar and huge sway when Gary Megson levelled matters early in the second half stays with me to this day. This after Cyrille raced through to fire us ahead with a blistering shot from the edge of the box. It looked as if Wednesday would press home their territorial advantage until Keith Houchen broke through twice to fire us into the semi-final and enabled me to have the following day off school with a sore throat. The pictures of the support behind Cyrille as he scores the opener are unprecedented. Sadly, scenes like that are not possible now following events there just two years after our visit. John Mullaney's We'll Be Back, detailing our first season post-Premiership, describes scenes experienced by his friends on the lower section of the Leppings Lane end. Lessons were clearly not learnt as hordes of fans descended upon the middle two blocks of terracing, thus squeezing desperate fans who climbed to safety near to us.

Boxing Day saw Dad, Mark, Adam and I freeze at the Ricoh as Ipswich took the points. The pre-match elation as guzzling fans on the concourse watched Chelsea surrender the lead to Reading with the most bizarre of own goals proved to be the only fun element of a rotten day. No Christmas cheer as yet again we lost on Boxing Day. Supporters are now beginning to turn against Micky and the team. With 20 games to go we lie 14th. A string of wins will catapult us back into the top half but I've been saying this all season and in seasons gone by. I'm resigned to the fact that if Bristol City dump us on our backsides the season will be over.

I'm sat here on 30th December. Just home from work, I just don't care any more. It's happening again, déjà vu, same old City. The last two games have been woeful. Only one point over the Christmas period and that against rock bottom Southend. With dad and Rich, Ade and Southend mates Ricki and Steve at the Ricoh there was no shortage of updates. Ade thoughtfully sums up my thinking tonight:

"Catch up in 2007 for some more crap football, U didn't miss much today."

Dad texted over our opener but even he couldn't be bothered to let me know the visitors had levelled. Jubilant Shrimpers fan Ricki sent over the depressing news, "One One"

There was no gloating, however. He sympathises with the Coventry supporter's plight. He's put up with me for the last eight years. Prior to the game he sent the message that we, as City fans, dread:

"Don't worry we have only won three times this season and none away. You will be under no pressure today."

Right. If a team's on a losing streak you can rely on us to end it. If a striker hasn't scored all season we'll provide a goodwill gesture. The game was Rich's first since the opening day. His rare appearance only irked him the more by our failure to entertain and win the game. Talksport had it nailed when they didn't bother sending a reporter for our game. We really are just making up the numbers.

The crowd today was 16,623. We're now back to the diehards. Defeat after defeat, poor performance after poor performance. The fickle bunch have gone away again. They've swallowed the hype and vehemently vomited it back where they knew it belonged. I've been to eight games this season and seen three on Sky, 11 out of 26 league games. Hereford in the cup I left to Ade. It's demoralising driving home after another defeat. I hope a cup run will inspire a return to form and the fortress re-established.

With less than a goal a game it's a world away from last season when goals flew in from all angles. This season McSheffrey has smashed 13 for his new employers before 2006 is out. On New Years Day we visit Leeds, marooned in relegation waters, managed by Dennis Wise. I can see the outcome crystal clear.

Avoiding Spurs was imperative for the semi-final. Leeds in a return to Hillsborough the reward and surely a meal ticket to Wembley. Remember, though, this is Coventry City. Nothing certain, nothing guaranteed. My joy at winning a weekend at the Bobby Charlton Soccer School was dampened by the realisation it was FA Cup semi-final day. The Coventry Evening Telegraph had set up a competition to coincide with our biggest-ever game. Having accepted a place on the course I had to miss out on Hillsborough.

Not all bad though, as the course was held at City's training ground at Ryton. Parents were dotted around the pitch where the masterclass was taking place, keeping us informed of events in Sheffield. One of City's least productive buys, David Rennie, opened the scoring for Leeds and the score remained the same approaching the 70-minute mark. Suddenly, car horns united around us as Micky Gynn slotted in the equaliser and Keith Houchen fired us in front with eight minutes to go. Lower division predator Keith Edwards turned cheers to jeers, sending the tie into extra-time. Dave Bennett's close range finish sent us to Wembley for the first time ever, to face Spurs.

Chapter 12

Rotten run continues

Driving back from a sodden New Year in Coventry, darkness was descending. Once the kids had dropped off and Emma immersed herself in Sudoku, Talksport again broke the news. *"Adam Virgo has levelled at Elland Road, it's 1-1."*

Not even a feature game for the second week running, this fixture in the nineties was renowned for goals galore. How times have changed; Leeds are doing even worse than we are and that's saying something. The half-time interval brought relief comparable to pre-season until around 4.10 when the agony continued with Leeds' winner.

Unloading everyone and their assorted Christmas presents into the house, my horror at my darling daughters seizing custody of the Sky remote saw me throw a minor tantrum. Unlike them, I refrained from lying on my back and kicking my legs in the air. When their programme finished at 4.50 it was straight back to Sky Sports News amid protestations, to see that nothing had changed and we'd lost again. I don't know why I bothered to switch back. I'd hoped looking over our shoulder was a thing of seasons past but now we're only eight points off the relegation zone. Five games unbeaten is now followed by five games without a win. The loan 'stars' have been dispatched and reserve centre-backs shipped out on frees. I'm worried about Bristol City in the cup. Having to work with City fans is bad enough. Following on from Sutton, Northampton and Rochdale, our tendency to flop when the going gets tough is well known.

In 1987, my fellow secondary school classmates suddenly

decided 'supporting' Liverpool and Manchester United from their armchairs and teletext remote controls was boring. They thought, *"Lets follow Coventry, they're doing well, we could even go to Wembley!"*

That's exactly what happened. The city went cup crazy. My mate Russell's mum queued for four hours to get us, season ticket holders, our prized £12 tickets. Flags and banners were everywhere, hanging out of windows and pubs. It really pissed me off these people were suddenly following my team.

At 3.23pm my 'phone vibrated continually:

*"What the f*** is going on?"* This came from City mate Steve stood ten rows in front of me in the rustic Wedlock stand at Ashton Gate.

"U wotchin Cov at Ashton Gate 2day?" Geordie Brian, never slow to dish out the verbals, was in his element here.

3-1 down to League One Bristol City was beyond my wildest nightmares. With an away following of just under 3,000 on FA Cup third round day, traditionally the biggest day of the season, the Sky Blue army were out in force. More notable for me was the half-hour drive to a City game. No trawling up the M5 with the family packed into the car and I was into the ground at 2pm.

Sat with Adam and old schoolmate, Matt, we were typically way too early, like you always seem to be for away games. Processed Nescafe warming the hands and a quick scout around to see who you recognise from days gone by. Out in force are old school mates, local work colleagues and paid up members of the Bristol Sky Blues. Trying to explain to your better half that just because the game is local there's no way you are leaving home at two is a tricky one that only the football supporter can really understand.

You know what happens when you cut it fine. The traffic jam and Saturday town traffic. The car breaks down. You dump it en-route and get into the ground late to be sat right behind a pillar. Then you're starving but don't want to miss any of the action in case City might score away from home.

Half-time saw the deficit reduced to one. A cracking cup-tie, the question on everybody's lips: can City come back from two goals down? The last time it happened was seven years ago. As darkness enveloped the ground the City contingent cranked up the incessant noise. Urging the team forward the support was terrific, some of the best I've sat amongst. The crossbar was rattled, corner after corner sent over to no avail. Wave of attack upon attack, but leaving ourselves open to counter attack. It really was an old-style tie, like football before the money revolution. The reaction when City's leveller arrived saw pandemonium on the terrace. Grown men leaping around, jumping all over each other. Pure elation and disbelief that City had pulled level. The sprint back to the stand from guys in the toilets, celebrating on the charge back to their seat. They missed the goal but shared in the moment, we don't get comebacks from 3-1 down at Coventry. The last ten minutes could have seen victory seized by either side but the terrific atmosphere was a joy to experience.

There was real support there today, fully behind the team. The away end was a sell out, a rarity for us with our perpetual poor form on the road. If only performances on the pitch at times could match the dedication behind the goal then the club would soar. The whole City support's thoughts were summed up by Ade. "*I never thought they had it in em!*"

We don't often get too much excitement at City games as we fall to our normal defeat. Three goals away from home is a bonus, the fact it was a cracking cup-tie made it all the better. Coming back to level in a bizarre kind of way felt like a victory of sorts. Laugh you may, but we just don't come back from two goals down. It's not in our make up, our character, to make it exciting for the loyal troops. In years gone by we shared a 5-4 with Forest and a league victory, 4-3 over Spurs on Boxing Day back in 1988. Yet we nearly lost them both.

The day had started with Dad's optimism soaring. "*Why are Coventry City like a tea bag? Because they only stay in the cup for a short time!"* The day ended with me arriving home just after 6pm on match day. It's taken ten years to see the Sky Blues on my now home turf. They didn't let me down. Monday morning at work I can raise my head high, no loss of face, my team fought back and showed character I, and numerous others, thought they didn't possess. I apologise for that thought.

***

For the first time ever, we travelled by coach to Wembley. I travelled with dad, Alan, Lee and Russ on a coach run by Coventry Schools FA. Commandeering the back seats like a school trip we refrained from rocking it as it went around tight bends and arrived at Wembley with three hours to spare. Soaking up the once in a lifetime atmosphere, we took our seats earlier than I'd ever done before. At Highfield Road we arrived ten minutes before kick-off.

There was plenty of pre-match entertainment available on cup final day. Options available to while away the time now include watered-down lager, reading the extortionate programme or watching the pre-match kick about. If you're really unlucky you get latched onto conversation by a solo fan itching for inane conversation. Alternatively you can attempt to decipher the clapped-out tannoy system. It's also a lottery who you get to sit next to. In my case, usually the group of five lads with four seats who jam their mate in along the line. You just know the longer towards kick-off the seat next to you remains empty the more likely the owner will be very pissed and needing a pee every ten minutes.

***

Back in 1980 City were hammered 5-0 by Everton at Highfield Road. 4-0 down at half-time, it was embarrassing even to a six-year-old. To this day it remains the worst home game I've ever seen although it now has a close rival. When we scored our two consolation goals today I didn't leave the comfort of the plastic seat. Didn't move a muscle.

Crystal Palace hit four goals with just under 40 minutes gone. 100 miles for this. Four attacks, four mistakes, four easy goals. 16,582 graced the arena, and many demanded the outer gates were opened, or refuelled for longer than normal on pasties and Carlsberg. I usually glance over at the away support because I'm envious of the success they're enjoying. Not this time. I sat stunned with feet up on the chair in front, scarcely moving except to shake my head in disbelief.

Stunned beyond repair I had to watch the painful repeat on Goals on Sunday to see who scored Palace's fourth. Yes, we hit the bar twice, but the realisation hit me that the players we've brought in are no better than the ones we had last year. Five defeats in the last seven has dropped us down to 16th place. We're eight points off the drop. On December 9th City were on the brink of the play-off zone.

A calamitous Christmas and New Year period has left us facing the kind of season run-in all too familiar in years gone by. Not too many fans were left at the whistle. Even the jeers were half-hearted, the energy and belief shattered. Operation Premiership has become a laughing stock. The club are victims of their own grand over-expectation. They even persuaded me that this could be the year. Finally there would be something to shout about.

Tonight, driving home from work, listening to the Monday Night Club on Five Live, we received a rare mention. City fans were invited to phone in to discuss our *"rotten run of form."* Fortunately, I arrived home before any City fans could reply. It's bad enough listening to the local phone-ins. The last thing I need is a national debate on the subject.

***

We were level with the corner flag and followed Houchen's header all the way. The scene behind Oggy's goal was a mass of sky blue. Flags and balloons were everywhere, ticker tape adorned the aisles, the fences obscured our view only slightly. The game was terrific. Only when we got home and watched it again did we realise just how good it was. Even now the skill levels and range of passing are great to observe. Motty was drooling in the commentary box with Jimmy Hill. Sir Trevor came off the fence, George and John laughed continually while Pleat knew a shock was on the cards.

Our journey home flew by in a cacophony of songs. We arrived home around 9pm, shattered, in time for Match of the Day. Next day the team toured the city. It took hours. Demand to see our triumphant heroes was unprecedented. We waited on New Union Street, then suddenly they were gone, into the hordes of fans/bandwagon jumpers.

***

8.29pm: *"1-0 down and playing like a bunch of school kids."*

8.30pm: *"Oh dear"*

8.37pm: *"Not looking good for Cov mate"*

9.02pm: *"Game over m8!"*

9.10pm: *"Bloody awful mate they are simply better than us."*

9.14pm: *"The Cov fans aren't happy! We do deserve it so far!"*

9.20pm: *"I think this has to be the worst city team in my lifetime. We're sinking like a stone in the league and out of both cups to lower league opposition."*

9.22pm: *"Oh dear its like a training session for Bristol City! I don't think Adams has long left!"*

9.41pm: *"2,600 fans there to see us go through that's a great turnout! Cov fans streaming out! Game over."*

9.45pm: *"What an embarrassment!"*

The Bristol Evening Post used the word 'swagger' to sum up Bristol City strolling to a 2-0 win at the Ricoh in the replay. The above texts rained in from a mixture of Coventry, Bristol City and neutral observers throughout the course of the game. Just three days after the Palace shambles, I'd no intention of going and have now sunk to a new low. Even relegation didn't feel as embarrassing and shameful as this result. Change has to come because we can't carry on as we are.

Having to live and work in the proximity of Bristol town centre, this is the worst result ever. When the draw was made we were eighth, five games unbeaten, progressing nicely. The fact that we lost abysmally adds to the humiliation. The manager carries the can as he buys the players who fail to perform. His purchases count him liable for results so the eight grand a week striker gets away scot-free.

The bus journey into work was peaceful, quiet, just me and my thoughts. Striding through the market adjacent to my office, coffee man Shaun began the tirade. Walking through the office even the girls who know nothing about football were taking the piss. The purchase of a packet of Lockets saw newsagent Martyn, a Rovers fan, roaring with laughter. It was taken on the chin. My time will come.

Talking to Steve, who attended the previous night's shambles, the word on his street was that Adams would be walking. At 11.05 the news flashed up on my phone during my lunch: "*Adams gone!*" In my angry, humiliated mind it was a relief that the axe had fallen. As the day progressed I began to sympathise with him. He saved us from relegation post-Reid and led us to eighth last season. However, the 12 players brought in during the close-season were the most afforded to any City manager in recent times and it's purely a results business. Sacked after 28 games is the same stage that Peter Reid was at two years ago. We just about survived then but a Herculean effort was required.

It will all come out in the wash. Patience will be required from us all but Adams did appear to lose the dressing room. There was little tactical bravery on show and little passion displayed in the touchline area.

Aged 12 you believe a precedent has been set. Surely if it was this easy we could repeat it year after year. The following season, 1987/88, Watford arrived in the fourth round after we cast aside Torquay. We were sent spinning out to a single goal defeat. The holders had exited in the fourth round. It was headline news.

Aged 32 a different slant is taken. We've reached a quarter-final (Sheffield United) yet lost to Northampton, Gillingham, Rochdale and the day Gander Green Lane will never forget, Sutton United. Only two years after the cup win, a defeat by a non-league team. Our most famous day was a brilliant experience, as was the defeat to Everton in the Charity Shield. That day we were backed by 51,000 fans. Where were they 14 years on as we tumbled out of the Premiership?

A bottle of '87 is one to be enjoyed, maybe it will never be repeated. It will never match the scenes experienced back then, unique, glorious times. My dad had waited 42 years for such a day. I hope I don't have to wait that long for a repeat or even a promotion campaign. A top six finish would be a start, but at the moment we have absolutely no chance.

With a weekend free prior to our fourth Sky appearance of the season there's been plenty of time for reflection. The club is a hive of activity with Adrian Heath as caretaker manager and fans voicing their opinions via newspapers and websites but no appointment made. Quite rightly they are taking their time. If the laughable Operation Premiership is to be believed the new managerial team will need to unite the club. I have no opinion on who'll be next in line but this is the 18th manager in my lifetime and it has to be the right one.

Each time the ball hit the net the Sydneyburger served up by Walkabout matched the fare served up by our troops – lifeless, with a hint of nausea. Comedy defending again saw three goals shipped while Ade, his brother Kieran and I sank into yet another negative haven. Sat a yard to my right was Plymouth diehard

Kalvin, a mate from work. He delighted in our agony, leaping on me on each occasion to celebrate our demise. Our initial reply to level matters saw backsides up off the comfy couches in celebration. The consolation strike in the 3-2 reverse saw little motion in any direction and a final 20 minutes where we failed to trouble a team who six seasons ago were in the lowest tier of the league.

I left the pub feeling no anger or frustration. It was just another day following the Sky Blues and a result to be expected. At least we couldn't fall any lower in the table. The following morning at work the talk was typically dismissive. Even the piss takers are getting bored. The January shopping window closes in just over a week and little activity seems to be happening chez Ricoh.

Oh yes I forgot, that's because we don't have a manager. Apparently over forty madmen have applied for the coveted position. So long as the poisoned chalice isn't presented with five games to go, with us firmly entrenched in the drop zone, I'll be happy. I've got to get more positivity from somewhere because this negative streak is really unlike me. I'm a confident, over-optimistic person usually, especially where City are concerned.

Being sat amongst the Ricoh faithful when a goal goes against us sees the boos immediately ring out. A negative mood prevails, with the odd exception such as that terrific day at Ashton Gate. I wish I could bottle that atmosphere and open it at the Ricoh. Away fans behind one of the goals, the whole side behind the dugouts is full of corporate fans, directors, Junior Sky Blues, media and club staff. The opposite side, where we sit, is superb, always full and the end to our right houses a loyal collection of City diehards. At Highfield Road City fans were behind both goals with visitors up in the stand.

The atmosphere at the Ricoh is very lopsided. Only two sides of the ground offer real support. Away fixtures provide a coming together of supporters with everyone united. It's a day out and everyone is fully behind the team. At home it's like cinema viewing - hard to rouse yourself, but it would help if there was some entertainment on offer.

Chapter 13

The revolving door

There's supposedly little room for sentiment in football yet over the years it's increased remarkably. The substitution of the player returning to his old club to enable him to receive a good-bye ovation not afforded due to the timing of the departure, the removal of a hat-trick hero to receive the adulation of the crowd before the fans have drifted out the ground with minutes to go, an old hero given an appreciative welcome time after time, a player subbed after returning from a long injury lay-off, the stalwart making his final appearance prior to hanging up the boots or, in our case, the parade of legends on the pitch prior to the last game at Highfield Road.

What's appreciated is the response from the player when he leaves the pitch, the team collectively applauding at the end of the game. What really aggravates is when the players leave the pitch after a defeat without paying homage to the masses, especially after away games when you've put in the miles to see a pile of dross served up. At home games the same few players applaud the three City sides of the ground, the same two or three clear off.

At Ashton Gate, shortly after scoring the leveller, Stern John turned and walked away from the fans all the way to the tunnel from 20 yards in front of us. It's not the first time he's done this, in fact he's one of the regular clear-off-the-pitch merchants. His sulk at home to Derby last year when he was refused a late penalty to seal his hat-trick typified his attitude. An average World Cup failed to raise his profile so he was stuck with us.

However, today we sold him to Sunderland, reclaiming the fee we spent two years ago. My abiding memory saw him ambling around on the halfway line while we were temporarily down to eight men against Crewe, everyone else closing down the opposition, he just labouring around the pitch. The sale is a good call.

***

Two weeks since the axe fell, still no appointment.

Coventry 1-0 Luton Town flashed up on my laptop with 18 minutes remaining. Finally, finally, a win, over a team as poor as us. My Dad's half-time summary captured the mood:

"When the conversation about my leaking loo is more interesting than the footy you know it's a poor game."

The longer the game dragged on the more I expected 1-1 to appear on the screen. A win is a win, at last. We climb no further in the table but improve the distance between ourselves and that dreaded dividing line separating third and fourth from bottom. The crowd of 18,781 looked impressive considering current form but the offer of a free ticket for every season ticket holder played a large part in avoiding the season's lowest gate.

Rather than looking at the higher echelons of the league table with 48 points up for grabs, the thought of a few wins strung together to take us away from the drop zone is more a hope than an expectation.

A Saturday free from work, but Sunderland away was never on the cards. Being in Coventry anyway saw us return from the Memorial Park with the clock on 3.20. As ever we were one down. I turned away from the screen and returned intermittently but at 4.20 we were still trailing so we headed for home. With CBeebies controlling the airwaves, our little dears soon dropped off and I elected for a surprise victory announcement when Tim Gudgeon announced the classified check on Five Live at 5pm.

Unbeknown to me Five Live had coverage of the Six Nations from Twickenham so it was over to Talksport, the station I've yet to hear announce us win since the demise at the Hawthorns. The tone of Talksport is significantly different to the revered Sports Report, with everything hurried along so it's hard to listen for your team's bad news. Our 2-0 defeat saw the channel instantly changed. I'd had enough.

I failed to see the winning strike against Luton, what with the late arrival of the pictures to Sky and having to be up for work in the morning. The Sunderland goals played out on Goals on Sunday now feature at the end of Championship highlights. How much lower can we go?

Six points clear of relegation with 15 to play. And still no new manager nearly three weeks on. Oh, also as an afterthought, our captain recently removed three front teeth from our vice-captain's chops after a tussle on the training pitch. All is rosy in the Sky Blue garden as our managing director sifts through the job applications now totalling 52. They must be crackers to even consider applying.

With the Six Nations taking up the airtime, relegating Final Score to the old Dukes Of Hazzard Saturday teatime slot and skytext knackered, this required a text to dad for updates on our clash with Cardiff. Vibrations would be the order of the day.

Euphoria with an early goal. A goal's rare in itself these days, an early one a collector's item. "*McKenzie 7 after good move*". Christ, if he wasn't scoring who would be?

The second vibration I took for half-time. Sadly, it wasn't. The amount of added time in each half nowadays means you're looking at near 50-minute halves. "*Cardiff pen in added time. Only Graham Poll knows why*".

We've had this on a few occasions, a Premiership referee officiating at one of our games. They invariably struggle, far more interested in their own profile. Personalities in their own rights nowadays, the game revolves around them. All then went quiet until, leaving the mobile on the kitchen table, it suddenly breakdanced across the fake mahogany and ground to a halt. Likewise, my heart rate:

"Behind 58 to well flighted long shot". This brought little reaction from me. I expected it.

More breakdancing followed. Crunch time, we've either levelled or sunk without trace.

"Cardiff down to 10 men, red card." Damn, in my experience this means 3-1 is on the cards.

How wrong could I be, little less than sixty seconds later, *"Adebola header 70"*. I'm just so used to things going against us that it's not cynicism but reality.

A busy afternoon saw yet more vibrations, now on a par with those electronic pads that stimulate the muscles around your knee after an operation, and this left me with a dilemma. The comeback is complete or we've been counter-attacked by the ten men and now trail. It was neither.

"Who's gonna be a daddy?"

Blimey, certainly not me! I've done my bit. Uni mate, another Rich, certainly picks his moments. Savouring a rare Watford victory at West Ham, he's on a stupendous high and this is great news. I then brought up the BBC1 in-screen score printer, more like 1987 than 2007 but it was the best resource I could find.

Individual scores flick through at snails pace, goals scored appear in yellow but it takes an age, especially as Scottish fixtures have ten minutes for half-time and invariably finish around 4.48. They're quickly followed by English non-league, then onto leagues one and two in England before at 4.56 our draw is finally confirmed.

For dad to tell me that we played really well and it was a really entertaining game, it MUST have been an exceptional performance. It's still one win in 12 and with teams below us closing the gap, there's only six points to the drop zone. I can feel repetition after each game simply due to the closeness of the teams in the lower half and the way we're sinking nicely.

∗∗∗

'*Three managers, two sackings and a relegation*' could quite easily title this book. On the day the board announced their interviews would commence for the vacant position the new incumbent was announced. Milne, Sexton, Gould, Mackay, Sillett/Curtis, Butcher, Howe, Gould back for more, Neal, Big Ron, Strachan, Nilsson, Gary Mac, Black, Reid, Adams and now Iain Dowie. He becomes the 18th manager in my 32 years. A bit of stability could be the meal ticket to a bit of success. I'm pleased, I think he'll do well and sort out our misfiring bunch. A modern manager, new fangled methods, his track record is impressive.

Perusing the Independent's write up of City's 3-0 shambles at Leicester the previous day, the vibrations started in earnest. "*Heath sacked*". No surprise there, he still carries Peter Reid baggage and the entire backroom staff have also been given the red card.

The previous day's third vibration by 3.27pm saw little flickering of emotion. "*Three down 27. Defence in shreds.*"

Fortunately for us the entire page two of teletext's occupants all failed to improve their position so we remain six points off the dreaded dividing line. 17 defeats out of 33 games, with Saints at home and Norwich away to follow this weekend, the fixtures now come thick and fast. No win in the next two and we could be on the shoulders of the bottom three or we could win both and leap into the top half of the table.

More pleasing is Dowie's number two, Tim Flowers. He played five games on loan for us back in the first season post-Premiership. He loved it, is a local lad and a supporter. If his passion and energy can rub off on this bunch of low scoring, goal-shipping near-millionaires, the good times may just be around the corner. But how many times have I said that? August was the last if I recollect.

My zest is rediscovered, I'd even go as far to say I'm excited by tonight's events. From what I've seen on Sky and heard from my spies at the game, we have a backroom team that gets involved in the game, displays energy and passion. Strachan jumped around arguing, Adams stood arms folded. Dowie and Flowers leap about, urge the side on, get involved in the action, celebrate with the supporters, unite the team. You've guessed it, we won! A 2-1 triumph over high-flying Saints takes us into the 40 points plus clump. Usually, the early vibration or *"Let's switch to the Ricoh Arena"* sees the bad news delivered at an early stage of the game, before 8pm. Rob McCaffrey's voice often tails off as he heads to the Ricoh for the news that's guaranteed to piss me off.

After flying through the five Thomas The Tank Engine bedtime reads, knowing the game had kicked off my voice quickened with each paragraph, the intrepid duo clocked this and thrust more literature in my direction. I couldn't refuse. By now, just shy of eight o'clock the yoga DVD had commandeered the wide screen, the internet temporarily crashed and there was a waiting text message. There was no holding back, straight into opening it up. I was braced for one of two scenarios: off to a flier as always happens with a new regime or same old same old, the new regime not had time to make an impact, the old manager's leftovers. *"Adebola four mins. Brilliant volley in off post."*

Begging the internet to get its act together for God's sake, finally it swung into life and Saints had levelled. No text from dad, only good news gets sent through from now on. Looking at the line-up, having been appointed only the previous day, Dowie has employed two right-backs down the right hand side to quell the threat of whizzkid Bale, who smashed that free-kick into our net back in August. That's correct, we're deploying tactical awareness. Unheard of, even I've twigged what we're trying to do. If this is a sign of things to come I'm impressed already.

Good Vibrations is the mindset I'm now in. I have to think positive, this guy is good, his track record is good, he talks about team spirit and iron will but as the sixth manager in six years I hope he stays around and works the miracle. The first impression is excellent:

"Kyle 29 brilliant header."

For my Dad to use the word 'brilliant' to describe our early strikes means either he's swept up in the euphoria or they really were crackers. Seeing them on the 10pm Sky Sports round-up, two things struck me. Firstly, we are headline news; we feature in the opening gambit. No longer does Sky show the score and scorers followed by no action as the pictures haven't reached the late evening show. We receive more airtime than any other Championship side, the fact we won is good enough but Dowie has raised our profile immediately. For once we aren't the last fixture to be shown. We also feature on teletext's main football menu. The normal format sees the top two sides receive the staccato headline; tonight that's us.

Secondly, the goals were pretty good. The most important thing was the fact that while I waited for the crucial next goal (we don't often get many of those) we held on for a massive victory. At the final whistle, all the players and management were on the field applauding the fans, instead of trundling off the pitch and applauding in small pockets. I've now cranked up my expectation levels; the vibe is good. Bring on Norwich away - can the new broom sweep us further up the table?

Momentum equals drive and impetus. In just six days the outlook has changed. Resilience, in the form of a rare away draw. Conceding with just minutes left on the clock, disappointed happiness is the name of the day. Receiving a write up in the Independent, along with Birmingham and Sunderland, the profile bar has been noticeably raised in such a small period of time. Our usual coverage sees us crammed into a rectangular slot, fifty words maximum. A rare Saturday afternoon with Sky Sports Saturday for company saw City's profile again raised. This time a featured match with their own reporter you could actually see, visible at the ground, Jeff Stelling's prompts to Carrow Road giving the result away.

Dowie's name is the key at present, an ex-Premiership manager with a large point to prove. Holding onto a single-goal lead for nearly forty minutes is an achievement for us, we just couldn't quite hold on until the end. Realising we're now 17 points off the play-offs with only 33 up for grabs, I'll settle for a rejuvenation and finishing the season on a high. Then, come the fixtures in June, expectation will crank up many notches and it'll be hopes raised all over again

It makes my 200-mile round trip pale into complete and utter insignificance. In recent weeks I've watched Sky Two's Football's Hardest Away Days, a feature on the lengths supporters go to follow their side. My Man City mate, Tony, commutes from Oxford over to Manchester many times during a season. Ade takes on the same journey up to the Ricoh as I do, his journey slightly longer. Featured on this programme was an East Fife fan who lives in Luton. Up at 6.30 on match day, a bus to Luton Airport, EasyJet to Edinburgh. Then two trains and two buses to Methil, in the middle of nowhere. A crowd of less than 500, all sat in the one stand, surrounded by sea. The previous week saw a Greenock Morton fan in Essex. He leaves home at 10.30 on the Friday night and collects his fellow Mortonian, who lives in Colchester. They drive through the night and arrive, nine hours later, at the ground. The crowd again low, the standard dire. After the game they stay in Morton until 4am then drive back through to Essex back in time for Sunday roast. How he can stay awake is one thing, the cost of the petrol unthinkable, family time must be non-existent. Oh, and I go every third Saturday. These guys go every week.

I haven't seen us play live since the Palace debacle in mid-January. With Ricoh contact established with dad and Adam, vibrations awaited, I was caught off guard at 3.05pm. With the wind of change at Coventry I'm now expectant every time the messages appear.

Quickly unlocking the phone to find out the early news I was stopped in my tracks with the simple message from Emma. *"Dish washer tabs please!"* For crying out loud! Not on a Saturday, not on match day!

Once I'd readjusted my match day karma it didn't take long for news to filter through from our home game with Hull:

"Doyle pen 20."

A simple enough message from dad, that's all that was required to leave a smile on my chops. We really are on a roll, the text saying that the crowd is 21,000 surprised me but at least it's on the increase. Come the West Brom game, the last one of the season, given the opposition's title promise, I reckon the doors will be locked.

After a quick load up of the respective teletext pages, 316, 317, 318, 319, vibrations returned with more good news:

"McKenzie 33 from Osbourne cross."

It's a revolution! Two wins and a draw in the three games has shifted the optimism, not for this season. This campaign ended when Bristol City dumped us out of the cup. Managing Director Paul Fletcher has announced plans to lower season ticket prices next season to draw in more punters, the cost of coach travel to away games has been halved to crank up the away following and next season away fans will move from behind the goal so we can claim back our rightful territory and use our support as a strength to aid the team rather than to let the opposition fill one end of our stadium and will their team on.

A rare purchase of a Sunday spread; I don't usually buy one when we're struggling. I don't need to read the paper to tell me what I already know, seeing us consolidated in 15th place on 45 points, ten off the relegation line. We're safe now, but if we hadn't picked up the last seven points we'd be firmly stuck in the lower reaches. The Dowie/Flowers effect has transformed the club, it's a shame there's only ten games left and we'll have to wait for the magic to take effect after a solid pre-season and some squad tinkering.

Pace and creativity has been outlined as a must, what is impressive is that the management are in tune with the fans, as we've been needing this for a long time. Also worth noting is our Hughes/Doyle midfield axis firing on all cylinders, a sudden rejuvenation, and the key point, what we've all agreed is the team are fitter and attack the second ball, a major previous weakness. We now compete across the middle. Amazing transformation, I can't wait for Barnsley at home in a fortnight.

Just a quick pointer, it's not just me that's been up and down this season, mirroring the team's fortunes. Man City fan Tony, feeling the misery after another hard slog from Oxford to Manchester on the glorious motorway networks, texted in his glum verdict:

"We will be playing you lot next year, we are definitely dropping".

At fourth bottom and six points clear of Charlton I think there are three far worse teams in the Premiership this season but they've sunk like a stone. If you remember it was Tony, five minutes after the fixtures were released, who said that if they didn't start well they'd be in trouble.

Six weeks ago the surprise packet of the season, Colchester, away, would have seen me give us zero chance of getting anything at all from the fixture. Now, a hard-won point in a goalless draw, four unbeaten, sees us fight and show resolve and determination not to lose. Sat at home (I'll be back at the Ricoh for the first time in two months next week), the superstitious diversion from Talksport to FiveLive Extra paid dividends.

With no Premiership programme due to FA Cup quarter-final day and only one evening cup-tie played today, FiveLive hosted a text competition where listeners could text in to influence which Championship fixture would be the live commentary game. Not surprisingly, we didn't feature in the vote and Leeds' relegation battle with Luton hogged the airwaves.

Interrupted at regular intervals to go *"around the grounds"* my initial thought was *"this is proper football without the nonsense of the Premiership"*. No diving, theatricals kept to a minimum, British players competing for the ball, proper fans roaring on their team, we're miles away from the Premiership but while our league is more enjoyable we all clamour to return there. As the only goalless fixture of the day we featured at the end of the round ups, yet since 20th February (St. Dowie's Day) I've felt good about things. The team is making the fans happy, the vibes are running around the city, there's belief at long last. Last time I saw us play live was the Palace debacle, when the Ricoh was a desperate place. My impending visit will be completely different, even more so if we turn over the rampaging Wolves who visit on the back of six straight wins.

With minutes to go I switched over to Final Score. Guess what? Typical. No Premiership programme, Six Nations on, where's Final Score? On at 5.20, that's where. With teletext having not moved on since 1985, I settled for Talksport's Final Whistle, hosted by Terry Christian and ex-Coventry legend Micky Quinn, with 606 delayed by the Middlesbrough v Manchester United cup tie. It was a delight to listen, as it was before the Premiership campaign began, to fans of lower division sides ranging from the Coventry fan on Coach Five praising our revolution, to Scunthorpe, Derby, West Brom and Sunderland.

Of course, as before, the odd Premiership fan can't leave the programme to us, they have to butt in on our show. Humour, rather than the usual whining, came from the West Ham fan who called in to say how nice it was for the Hammers not to lose on a Saturday. Quality. And by the way, we're up to 14th, 11 points off the drop but not safe yet.

Expectation: assumption, belief, probability, likelihood. We've turned full circle. A fifth game unbeaten, third home victory on the bounce, the same squad of players who plumbed the depths of mid-December/January and most of February have rejuvenated, probably through the man-management and tactical astuteness of our new leader. I bet they can't believe how well they've started, it almost now makes a defeat acceptable.

To defeat Wolves, themselves on the back of six straight wins, to win a Midlands derby for a change, is a massive upturn. Having ensured the kids were tucked up in time for kick-off and with no chance of getting to the game with a wife at work while

I wasn't (shame all the home midweek games are on Tuesdays; Wednesday would suit me better) we featured as one of the four main games with a live studio panellist, Tony Gale, sat next to Peter Reid. His first comment of note was to inform that the kick off was delayed due to crowd congestion. How I laughed! I envisaged a monster attendance, higher than the 27,000 for the Birmingham defeat. When it came in as 22,099 it boiled down to disbelief at how disorganised City are with larger than normal attendances.

It's as if a run of poor form, with lower attendances, makes it easier for the club. Little congestion, no queues, nice and simple. For an evening game against local rivals people are rushing to the ground from work, a huge number converging on the same place at the same time. They cope in the Premiership but then they've had plenty of practise. Highfield Road, with a capacity of 22,000, never encountered delays to games. What happens if, against West Brom, 30,000 turn up? Unless they learn quickly and start to plan for big crowds we'll never be able to host top-flight football.

Anyway, it kicked off at 8.05. The game, not the local rivalry. The vibe felt good. Normally when Rob McCaffrey builds in a goal you can sense it's gone against us. This time it was different. When Wolves went down to ten men just before half-time Mr Negative resurfaced as I turned to Emma and said "*You watch this we'll concede now, Sod's law*", which is exactly what happened. Our domination was reiterated on every occasion Tony Gale was brought into the shot until the glorious scoreline appeared in front of me **Coventry 2-1 Wolves**.

At 9.54, along with Sunderland v Stoke, we were the only games still in progress. The word "*Goal!*" rang out from the panel. My heart skipped a beat and jumped a mile. Not now, surely, not against ten men. It took a quick switch to channel 402, Sky Sports Two, to allay the fears. The word had been uttered by Peter Reid, not Tony Gale. The whistle finally sounded at 9.59. Still 14th but there's daylight now with the slight chance of returning to page one of teletext. Unfortunately, it's a bit too late in the season but we're on the right tracks, united at last.

Chapter 14

The once a season performance

13th January saw a shambolic performance at the Ricoh. Four goals in the first 39 minutes and Crystal Palace rocket into a four-goal lead while I sat there, stunned. How things have changed. The day started well, the Scenic oiled and watered, lattes and baby chinos consumed amidst a throng of Cardiff fans en route to defeat at Derby. Roadworks on the main ring road and the pace stepped up as we reached the ground with ten minutes to spare. Fortunately, Barnsley at home provided no turnstile queue potential and we took our seats in the now-named Tesco Stand with the sun beating down, our view along the edge of the penalty area unparalleled.

I noticed a difference immediately. An active dugout for a start, involved in the game, passionate about what they're doing. The players fought for every ball, passed into space, moved into positions, attacked the second ball, played with pace, united the crowd. Three goals in the first half, taken superbly, created by intelligent, thoughtful approach play, saw a standing ovation at half time.

You might think the above comments are a bit strange but I've only described them as I see them because in the past we haven't done the basics well. The team looked fit, organised, man-managed and, most importantly, coached. It was as if we were watching another team because the way City played wasn't like what we've been used to in the past. It's other clubs whose managers show imagination, creation, common sense and tactical awareness. Other clubs demonstrate the kind of football witnessed today. I'm gobsmacked.

The same group of players so abject in December/January have been motivated and coached to perform in such a way that we feel invincible and will win every game we play. The key word is expect. I expect us to turn every side over now but with a different belief that I had pre-season. There's something different here.

The game also saw the only ever occasion I've missed a goal at a live game. At 4-0 up I experienced that once a season treat where you sit back and enjoy the moment. I enjoyed it so much I followed the Mexican wave around the ground, even the corporates took part, and looked for the response from the away support as it motored towards them. They joined in, erupting with delight as they scored at the precise moment the wave hit their end. The sheer opportune timing of the wave reaching the away end with the ball being, apparently, headed in from a corner, you couldn't put a price on. At least it wasn't a City goal I missed.

The game petered out, a little like the 3-0 win over Norwich earlier in the year. This time the crowd stayed until the end, the reason apparent as the players all applauded us. Along came Dowie and Flowers to salute the crowd, receiving and giving applause which, I can tell you, is much appreciated. It's a nice habit to get into, winning. Text communication was non-existent today, they only come alive when we lose, so I gloated with texts a-plenty, savouring the moment.

After the barren spell of Christmas and New Year I never expected a renaissance like this; the turnaround is unbelievable, miraculous. We now have a fortnight break due to the international boredom and with only seven games remaining, the season has again flown by. It's finishing at the wrong time, we're now the form team. Yes us, the form team! And I'm no longer looking over my shoulder at the foot of the table and following other team's results. The focus has shifted back to our team and our team only.

Back in the gloom of New Year Birmingham away was one game I feared. The spring renaissance has changed my view, there's optimism now that we can get something out of the fixture. Not shared by Ray Stubbs it seems. During the Final Score table updates he pronounces. *"Birmingham will go second when they play Coventry tomorrow."* Cheek.

The reason the fixture was to be played on Sunday 1st April, April Fools' Day and my seventh wedding anniversary, was police 'advice' as it's a local derby. Attendance at St. Andrews was a non-starter for the aforementioned reason, having to rely on Teamtalk for text updates at 25p a message the only way I could keep in touch with events. With a 2.00 kick off I was rather confused by the initial message at 1.30. I needn't have worried, sending me the team news was a nice thought and appreciated. While out and about the vibration didn't feel a good one, and so it proved. Two more bad news texts confirmed a 3-0 reverse, honeymoon over for our new leader.

Watching the goals around midnight on Football League Review provided a minor consolation. Even though we shipped three and failed to score, it was sloppy more than anything else. Our recent rejuvenation has raised all our hopes, a shame we couldn't get something out of the game with the City fans packed in behind the goal in their thousands, having shelled out £30, yes 30 notes for a ticket. Extortion must be the middle name of the Birmingham board, what a rip off. If the plan was to dissuade City fans from travelling it may have worked under Micky Adams but not now.

With 40 games played, six remain and we've lost 18, nearly half our fixtures. Now on 52 points the bottom side, Luton, have 37. It's a good job our form has improved because if we'd continued in the same vein I fear for how low we could have fallen. League One without a doubt. One more win will make sure.

And still we seek that win. On Easter Saturday we gunned the Scenic up the M5 for the last family football visit of the season. The roads were clear seeing as we have no beach anywhere near the Midlands. With little motorway traffic around, a stream of Sky Blue filtered its way into the ground with a very vocal QPR contingent roaring on their once entertaining Premiership, now relegation-threatened, outfit. They battled for every ball and defeated us hands down in the physical stakes, scoring with their only attempt on target, albeit at the third time of asking after two superb reaction saves from our player of the year in waiting. It sums up the season when your goalkeeper has domi-nated the vote. Not since Steve Ogrizovic have we had a depend-able stopper and Andy Marshall certainly fits the bill.

At the final whistle our visitors rejoiced at three extremely vital points to lever them away from the relegation zone. Our heroes stood stunned. Not one of them moved. They couldn't believe they'd lost. It was like watching back in January and February. Jekyll and Hyde is featuring prominently at such an important time of the season.

The Easter period is traditionally the time when a number of promotion and relegation issues are decided. Although the league table doesn't lie it would take something to go badly wrong now for all the sides below us to pick up maximum points and for us to lose each fixture. Our final games of this mostly tortuous campaign see us up against Derby, Preston and West Brom, all in the top six with something to play for. We've now taken the role of spoilers in our division. Instead of rolling over we've triumphed against the likes of Wolves and Southampton, throwing the proverbial spanner in the way of their play-off charge. Then defeats handed out to Barnsley and Hull have pushed them further to the dreaded divided line above the bot-tom three.

A point at top of the table Derby continued the spoiling theme. Driving home shortly after 4.30 on Easter Monday, Five Live cut from its live Premiership coverage to pan to Pride Park. Only because we were up against the leaders did we have a live link. Normally we feature in a quick goal flash for no more than ten seconds. Today the prompt summed up our position in media thinking: *"And its not gone the way you might expect."*

Basically we had, shock of horrors, taken the lead. Just six minutes later the scores were level and fear of defeat then crept into my thoughts after being 17 minutes from a shock victory away from home. Our first potential away win since 25th November and today it's 9th April. That's why we're in the bottom half. With 13 defeats on the road only Leeds have lost more and they're going down.

Fortunately, we can win at home on a fairly regular basis. For the sixth season running since relegation we've failed to make the play-offs and for four out of those six seasons we've finished in the lower half. It's a good job Mr Dowie took the job when he did otherwise we could well have been looking at visits to Cheltenham and Port Vale.

Quiz question: have we scored from a free kick this season? I don't think we have but I'll check. It's a fact that won't have been lost on our new regime.

A day in work with Preston the visitors. Brother Rich ventured to the game for the first time this year. His last game was Southend at home in December, work and location have knackered his season. The fact that Talksport has jinxed me didn't put me off. One down after seven minutes when they panned to our game I could hear the roar and tried to work out who was cheering. Alas, the reporter beat me to it. 0-1.

Ten minutes later there was no need to even find out who had scored. 0-2 graced the airwaves. When you hear the prompt *"Off to the Ricoh"* you know there's been a goal. Heading off to a Premiership game it's for an update on the action. Lower league games give goal information then it's back to the studio to catch up on the 'real' action in the elite division. Back to the action. I plugged back in to hear *"Coventry 0 Preston 4"* after 56 minutes. Talk about swings and roundabouts.

It was more interesting following the fortunes of the teams challenging for promotion or fighting off relegation. I really wish the season would just end now. Once the last final whistle blows the stress of following City will disappear will be replaced by the anticipation of who'll be signing in the summer months. The fixtures will be released in mid-June and then the expectation levels will rise again as they do each and every pre-season.

To cap it all the horse I had pulled out in the Grand National sweep fell at the first fence. When the final whistle blew today it signalled euphoria and ecstasy for Scunthorpe, Hartlepool and Walsall. On the contrary there was doom and gloom for Rotherham and, more damaging, Torquay, who dropped out of the league into the Conference after more Houdini escapes than us down the years. It will be especially difficult for them to get back. The quality of Conference football is improving all the time and Dagenham & Redbridge, newly-promoted, will do well next season.

Now our home form is on the wane. With the second-worst away record (this is becoming a bit of habit now) in the division we've lost seven at our very own fortress. Watching Final Score you can hear the joy and jubilation drowning out the reporters at each of the promotion venues as the celebrations begin. I sit there shaking my head as we're still not safe from relegation. Eight points above Leeds with nine to play for. We'd be down if we hadn't had that unbeaten run when Dowie arrived. Thank God he did.

I spoke to Rich. He was as fed up as I felt. Nothing positive to say at all. Can the last one out turn off the light?

Chapter 15

Just like it always is

We haven't scored from a free-kick this season. This may explain why when we're faced with a golden opportunity to score, our lack of creativity and invention rears its ugly head. All we've seen are ferocious shots rebounding off the wall or nestling in Row Z. Sides pushing for promotion are renowned for having a creative genius up their sleeve. Our magician's wand has gone missing.

So has Don Hutchison. His absence since the middle of November hasn't helped our fortunes, we've missed him more than we think. The ability to slow down the pace of the game or to thread a sublime defence-splitting ball has been sadly lacking. You can't put a price on experience.

Another defeat, this time at Hillsborough, leaves us with one point from the last 15. It's like the start of the season all over again. Listening to our demise after drawing level, the lack of feedback on our game saw me draw the conclusion that we had meekly surrendered again.

I apologise for my initial response. Reading the reports later, we actually did something very difficult in the course of a game of football. Striking the post with two minutes to go the rebound fell straight to Kevin Thornton. His snapshot slammed against the opposite post and out for a goal kick.

No-one relayed any comments to me after the game, no-one. We are now completely insignificant in every single football fan's eye. Luton were relegated today after just two years in the Championship. The key reason they've gone down is because they're a selling club and have lost their star players. Where have we heard that before? It's why the gulf exists between the small clubs and those pushing for promotion back to the promised land. These clubs have the clout to pick the star players of the smaller teams; witness Birmingham signing McSheffrey. The pickings are too good to resist and the small clubs know the money will help secure their futures.

On the Sunday after the match I gamely stayed up past midnight to watch the Football League Review, expecting us to be on in the first quarter of an hour. Instead I'm made to wait. Leagues one and two take the priority and even the goals summary show has us as an afterthought.

My mind flashes back to my pre-season thoughts on the chances of our rivals. *"Brum will struggle"* is my biggest faux pas. They'll soon secure automatic promotion after beating us twice on the way. McSheffrey has scored 15 goals since his transfer and landed up in the PFA Championship Team Of The Year.

Watford failed to survive one season in the top division as their fate was sealed. The positive for me is Rich lives close to Watford and the meet is on, an awayday special to be planned. City always travel well to Vicarage Road but the team don't. A change of fortune on the road needs to be addressed before the glory days following the Sky Blues return.

The final home game of the season is always a special occasion. The fans salute their heroes, the players tour the pitch after the final whistle and the Player Of The Year award is presented. City, in recent years, have stopped presenting the trophy on the pitch and hand it over to the lucky recipient at a black tie affair in a local hotel. So having forked out for a season ticket you must splash out further to witness the presentation of the trophy to our hero. There's something not right here. It's voted for by the fans so we should see the lucky recipient get his hands on the coveted goblet.

With dad in Spain the chance for a gents day out presented

itself. Loading Ade, brother Kieran and mate Tim (Liverpool fan with a Scouse burr) into the Scenic and minus Emma, Aimee and Jolie we headed north. Removing Cbeebies from the entertainment system we headed back to the Madchester era with the Stone Roses, Happy Mondays and acid house compilations adorning the airwaves. Rolling up at the Three Horseshoes and leaving it in the car park for the duration of the match we cut through the local streets and straight into the fish and chip auditorium. My first scallop for ten years and large chips battered into submission ensured I was stuffed prior to kick-off, with indigestion forthcoming.

We nearly didn't make it. Usually I'm the passenger on the way to matches. Today saw three wrong turns at roundabouts en route to a ground I've visited on numerous occasions. The laughter in the back had just about subsided as we parked up and fed £3 into the hand of the car minder.

A minute's applause for the late Alan Ball was something else. The sight of over 26,000 people applauding in unison was a fitting tribute and observed superbly by all present. I saw him play live only once, back in 1982 when City beat a Saints side also featuring Channon and Keegan 4-2.

Present in the away end were 6,000 West Brom supporters, hence the reason why next season away fans will be moved from behind the goal. You may as well give them a goal start, it's such an advantage.

Prior to kick-off our 'keeper Andy Marshall collected the player of the year awards from the supporters' clubs. It sums up the season, he missed a number of games through injury over Christmas and still triumphed. As the game kicked off the referee was clocked by me. Chris Foy, a Premiership referee. Someone who feels he's above us and will want to be the centre of attention. My hunch was correct as he sent off Ben Turner for nothing more than a yellow card offence. It was so ridiculous Turner, making his home debut, received a standing ovation as he left the pitch.

Such referees belittle the lower league players with their behaviour. A week later I saw Mr Foy as fourth official at both the Manchester derby and Arsenal v Chelsea. That's where he would prefer to be because it's what he's used to. At the end of the game we didn't hang around after another single goal defeat. Usually I stay to applaud the lap of 'honour' but felt so miffed by the season I've just witnessed that we left and headed for the club shop. There was nothing of interest in there and I refrained from giving them any more of my hard-earned.

We stopped for a quick pint in the Three Horseshoes then headed home with 606 peppering the airwaves. I was tempted to call in about the standard of refereeing but by 6pm my anger had subsided and I just listened to others venting their spleen. Nestling now in 18th position we've lost eight at home and 14 on our travels. We're seen as a rollover, not just in other teams' eyes but in mine also.

As the season draws to a close relegation and promotion issues are decided and we play no part in any of them. When we tumbled out of the Premiership the only team worse than us, statistically speaking, was Bradford. Six years on they'll be starting next season in the old division four. Profligate spending during their top-flight era has plummeted the club into the position they now find themselves in. It could well have been us, and it's a harsh lesson to learn from. Of course, the people involved back in 2001 are no longer involved with the club and the present incumbents are left to pick up the pieces.

Southend dropped back into league one and my prediction on their season has come true. After a good start they went on a bad run and failed to get out of the bottom three again. Scunthorpe are mirroring Southend's progress with two rapid promotions and they'll face the same problem next season. As Derby failed to win at Palace, Sunderland and Birmingham were promoted to the promised land. So much for my prediction that Blues would struggle, and Sunderland's renaissance under Roy Keane has been nothing short of remarkable. When we beat them on the opening day they caved in. What happened there is amazing. For two of last season's relegated teams to return immediately is some going and an admirable feat. The third, West Brom, eventually fell to rejuvenated, and unlucky not to go up anyway, Derby in the play-off final at brand new Wembley.

Chapter 16

Full time

The day prior to the final fixture Leeds went into administration, took the ten point penalty on the chin and dropped into the third tier of the Football League for the first time ever. It could have been us in seasons gone by, we've been lucky not to fall further through the league system. Bristol City finally returned to the Championship after eight years away. Good news for me with Ashton Gate half an hour from home, so we can finally show them how to play football after this season's cup debacle.

I anticipated us losing at Burnley. Negative yet again, we've not beaten them at Turf Moor since we've been in this division. With a one o'clock kick off Sky Sports featured on who out of Sunderland and Birmingham would be crowned champions and who would claim the three remaining play-off spaces to line up alongside Derby. Funnily enough, 18th against 16th just about attracted a reporter at the game. While ensuring one of my daughters was firmly occupied throughout the 90 minutes to prevent her from pressing the 'off' button on the wide screen, I flicked between Preston, Birmingham and the Sky Sports Special, live in the studio, rolling scores programme. Twice I left the room to go into the kitchen and twice we scored.

The shock stunned me for ten minutes before Burnley pulled one back. Here we go again, but surprisingly we won. Our first away win since QPR on the 25th November puts the jinx firmly to bed. We managed to scrape up to a final placing of 17th. Dreadful, absolutely dreadful yet again.

P46 W16 D8 L22 F47 A62 P56

Six years have now been spent in this league. Time is moving on. The Premiership is moving further and further away from the rest. Charlton joined Watford in the Championship for next season as their relegation was confirmed. As the Premiership season concluded a week later, Sheffield United, always one of our tricky opponents in seasons past, dropped through the trap door after a winner takes all defeat at home to Wigan. I have mates who follow each of the relegated sides. As the curtain closed only Aidan tendered a response, having predicted a lack of quality would scupper Charlton's hopes back in August. "*Nails going in the coffin for the cafc!*" He was spot on with his prediction.

Manchester City's Tony trailed back from a final home defeat of the season having predicted trouble if the first six games of the season failed to bring any reward. His misery is there for all to see:

"*Just caps a truly miserable season*".

Forest fan Matt has expected promotion having won the first four games on the spin. Finishing in fourth and a play-off duel with Yeovil drew a considered response:

"*Play-offs here we come what a shame!*"

After throwing away a two-goal first leg lead to lose 5-2 at home his emotions changed somewhat:

"*I'm devastated. Threw it away.*" Too right they did. Visits from Bristol Rovers, Walsall and Hartlepool await.

Did anyone enjoy the season? I certainly didn't and don't know a Coventry supporter that did. We sold three strikers: McSheffrey's form and exploits are well documented. Stern John also achieved promotion with Sunderland, notching valuable goals along the way. Andy Morrell completes the trio with 20 for Blackpool en route to playing us next season in the Championship after their play-off success. This guy was regularly stuck out of position by all the City managers he played under after notching 46 for Wrexham prior to his arrival.

Our leading scorer tallied nine as we finished as the second lowest scorers in the league after Leeds. Three weeks after our season ended the play-off finals were in full swing and it was great to watch the kind of football we're crying out for at Coventry.

While finishing this chapter I await to see who will be released as the Dowie/Flowers combination works its magic to entice winners to the club. Expectation levels will be raised once again as the season approaches and we'll all be hoping for that dream season where we sweep all before us. Let's hope it won't be a case of January and the season's over once again.

Also available from Heroes Publishing

HUNDRED WATTS
a life in music
by RON WATTS

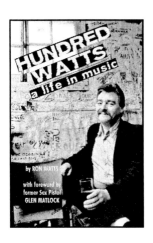

With Foreword by former Sex Pistol
Glen Matlock

Ron Watts remains one of the most influential men in
the history of British music.
From John Lee Hooker to Johnny Rotten, Bowie to Bono,
Ron got to know and work with the biggest and the best.
From bringing Blues greats to Britain, to his central role
in the 1976 Punk Festival at London's legendary 100 Club,
he helped shape youth culture in the UK.
Hundred Watts is the informative, revealing and extremely
funny account of his days at the cutting edge
of the music business.
Price – £7.99
ISBN – 0954388445

Also available from Heroes Publishing

HERBERT CHAPMAN
the first great manager
by SIMON PAGE

The son of a bare-knuckle fighting coal miner, Herbert
Chapman became the most famous football manager of his day.
One of the game's true immortals, he took Northampton Town,
Leeds City, Huddersfield Town and Arsenal to heights few had
ever dreamed possible. Yet his career nearly ended when he
was handed a lifetime ban in one of the game's earliest, biggest
and most notorious "bungs" scandals.
Including never before published family photographs and
stories, this book looks at the life of the man who stands at the
head of the list of English football's foremost bosses; the
forerunner of Busby, Shankly, Paisley, Clough and Ferguson –
the first great manager.

Price – £9.95
ISBN 0954388453 – EAN 9780954388454

HEROES PUBLISHING
PO Box 1703, Perry Barr, Birmingham, B42 1UZ
www.heroespublishing.com